TAKS Spiraled

World Geography

Texas Consultant
Karen Moorhead
Corpus Christi Independent School District
Corpus Christi, Texas

McDougal Littell
Evanston, Illinois • Boston • Dallas

Printed in the United States of America

ISBN 0-618-15504-x

5 6 7 8 9 - BHV - 05

Contents

TAKS
Quick Prep

Quick Prep

This Quick Prep section provides a handy reference to key facts on a variety of topics in world geography.

Major Geographic Features by Region

United States and Canada
Appalachian Mountains, Rocky Mountains, Continental Divide, Canadian Shield, Great Plains, Mississippi River, Mackenzie River, Great Lakes, Gulf of Mexico
Latin America
Andes Mountains, Sierra Madre, Brazilian Highlands, Guiana Highlands, llanos, pampas, Amazon Plain, Amazon River, Orinoco River, Paraná River
Europe
Alps Mountains, Pyrenees Mountains, Apennine Mountains, Balkan Mountains, *Massif Central, Meseta,* Northern European Plain, Scandinavian Peninsula, Jutland Peninsula, Iberian Peninsula, Italian Peninsula, Balkan Peninsula, Danube River, Rhine River, Baltic Sea, Mediterranean Sea, North Sea
Russia and the Republics
Ural Mountains, Caucasus Mountains, Tian Shan, Central Siberian Plateau, Kamchatka Peninsula, Northern European Plain, West Siberian Plain, Turan Plain, Kara Kum, Kyzyl Kum, Ob River, Yenisey River, Lena River, Volga River, Lake Baikal, Caspian Sea, Aral Sea, Black Sea, Baltic Sea
Africa
Atlas Mountains, Ahaggar Mountains, Mount Kilimanjaro, Mount Kenya, Ethiopian Highlands, Great Rift Valley, Sahara, Libyan Desert, Kalahari Desert, Namib Desert, Nile River, Congo River, Niger River, Zambezi River, Victoria Falls, Lake Tanganyika, Lake Victoria, Red Sea, Mediterranean Sea
Southwest Asia
Zagros Mountain, Elburz Mountains, Taurus Mountains, Hejaz Mountains, Hindu Kush Mountains, Golan Heights, Arabian Peninsula, Anatolian Peninsula, Tigris River, Euphrates River, Jordan River, Dead Sea, Red Sea, Persian Gulf, Black Sea, Bosporus Strait, Dardenelles Strait, Straits of Hormuz
South Asia
Himalaya Mountains, Mount Everest, Hindu Kush Mountains, Karakoram Mountains, K2, Vindhya Mountains, Western Ghats, Eastern Ghats, Deccan Plateau, Northern Indian Plain, Thar Desert, South Asian Peninsula, Indus River, Ganges River, Brahmaputra River, Arabian Sea, Bay of Bengal
East Asia
Kunlun Mountains, Qinling Shandi Mountains, Mount Fuji, Manchurian Plain, North China Plain, Gobi Desert, Taklimakan Desert, Korean Peninsula, Tarim Basin, Huang He (Yellow River), Chang Jiang (Yangtze River), Xi Jiang (West River), Yalu River, Yellow Sea, Sea of Japan, East China Sea, South China Sea
Southeast Asia, Oceania, and Antarctica
Mainland: Annamese Cordillera, Indochinese Peninsula, Malay Peninsula, Mekong River *New Zealand:* Southern Alps *Australia:* Great Dividing Range, Murray River, Great Barrier Reef *Antarctica:* Transantarctic Mountains

World Climate Regions

Climate	Features	Location
Tropical Wet	• consistently hot, humid, and rainy	• tropical areas of Latin America, Africa, and Asia
Tropical Wet and Dry	• warm, rainy summer and cool, dry winter	• next to tropical wet climate regions in Latin America, Africa, and Asia
Desert	• less than ten inches of rain per year; hot deserts are hot during the day and cool at night' coo/cold deserts have warm to hot summers and cool to cold winters	• hot deserts: tropical and middle latitudes of all continents except Antarctica • cold deserts: mid-latitudes of Northern Hemisphere, often in the rain shadow of mountains
Semiarid	• about 18 inches of rain per year; hot summers and mild to cold winters	• interior of continents or in a zone around deserts
Mediterranean	• hot, dry summer and cool, rainy winter	• around the Mediterranean Sea, west coast of the United States and Chile, southern parts of Australia and Africa
Humid Subtropical	• long, hot, and humid summer and mild to cool winter	• southern United States, large areas of China and South Asia, eastern coast of Australia, east central South America
Marine West Coast	• constant moderate temperature; evenly distributed precipitation throughout the year; frequently cloudy, foggy, and damp	• west coast of North America, most of Western Europe, southwestern coast of South America, southeastern coast of Africa, southeastern coast of Australia, New Zealand
Humid Continental	• great variety in temperature and precipitation; four seasons	• mid-latitudes of the Northern Hemisphere
Subarctic	• short, cool summers and long, very cold winters; precipitation averages less than 20 inches per year	• upper middle latitudes of Northern Hemisphere
Tundra	• cold with little precipitation; summer lasts only a few weeks and temperature rises only slightly above 40°F	• around the Arctic Circle
Highland	• varies with latitude, altitude, topography, and continental location; generally cooler than lowlands of same latitude and greater temperature range between day and night; generally more precipitation on lower, windward slopes	• mountain ranges of North America, South America, Europe, Asia, and Africa
Icecap	• snow, ice, and permanently freezing temperatures with little precipitation	• Greenland and Antarctica

Extreme Places and Regions

Feature	Place or Region	Description
Hottest Place	• Al Aziziyah, Libya	• 136°F on Sept. 3, 1922
Coldest Place	• Vostok Station, Antarctica	• –128.6°F on July 21, 1983
Wettest Place	• Mount Waialeale in Hawaii	• average annual rainfall of 460 inches
Driest Place	• Africa, Chile	• average annual rainfall in one 59-year period was 3/100 inch
Highest Mountain	• Mount Everest in Nepal	• rises 29,035 feet above sea level
Lowest Place On Earth	• Dead Sea in Israel	• 1,349 feet below sea level
Longest River	• Nile River in Africa	• 4,180 miles long
Highest Waterfall	• Angel Falls in Venezuela	• 3,212 feet high
Deepest Lake	• Lake Baikal in Russia	• more than a mile deep
Largest Lake	• Caspian Sea in Central Asia	• covers 143,250 square miles
Longest Freshwater Lake	• Lake Tanganyika	• in east-central Africa 420 miles long
Largest Island	• Greenland	• 839,999 square miles
Largest Desert	• Sahara in northern Africa	• 3.5 million square miles
Largest Glacier	• Malaspina Glacier in Alaska	• 840 square miles
Largest Supply of Fresh Water	• Antarctica ice sheet	• volume of 7.25 million cubic miles
Most Earthquakes	• Ring of Fire	• About 80 percent of the world's major earthquakes occur here.
Most Active Volcanoes	• Ring of Fire	• About 60 percent of the world's active volcanoes are found here.
Most Tornadoes	• Texas	• Between 1950 and 1994, the state was hit with 5,490 tornadoes.
Most Snowfall in 24-hour Period	• Silver Lake, Colorado	• On April 14–15, 1921, about 76 inches of snow fell in 24 hours.
Most Rainfall in One Minute	• Unionville, Maryland	• On July 4, 1956, more than an inch of rain fell in one minute.
Most Rainfall in One Year	• Cherrapunji, India	• From August 1860 to July 1861, about 1,042 inches of rain fell.
Strongest Winds	• Mount Washington, New Hampshire	• On April 12, 1934, a gust of wind blew 231 miles per hour.
Largest Hailstones	• Coffeyville, Kansas	• The hailstone measured 17.5 inches in circumference and fell on September 3, 1970.

Major Cities by Region

City	Population*	Notable Fact
United States and Canada		
Toronto, Canada	2,540,100	• banking and financial center
New York City, United States	8,056,200	• one of the most important centers of trade and culture in the world
Latin America		
Mexico City, Mexico	8,578,300	• built on the site of the Aztec capital of Tenochititlan
Rio de Janeiro, Brazil	5,939,500	• one of the most spectacular natural settings in the world
Caracas, Venezuela	1,784,800	• one of the most modern Latin American cities
Bogotá, Colombia	6,540,400	• sits on a plateau about 8,660 feet in elevation
Lima, Peru	7,451,900	• cultural center of Peru
Buenos Aires, Argentina	11,624,000	• home to about one-third of Argentineans

City	Population*	Notable Fact
Europe		
London, England	7,341,400	• dates back nearly 2,000 years
Paris, France	2,115,400	• considered one of the most beautiful cities in the world
Berlin, Germany	3,317,000	• a symbol of the Cold War when it was divided into Communist and non-Communist districts
Rome, Italy	2,646,700	• an important center of civilization for more than 2,000 years
Athens, Greece	759,100	• birthplace of Western civilization
Madrid, Spain	2,894,100	• home to the Prado, one of the world's greatest art museums
Warsaw, Poland	1,611,800	• rebuilt after its nearly total destruction in World War II
Russia and the Republics		
Moscow, Russia	8,383,000	• layout takes the shape of a wheel with the Kremlin at the city's historic center
Kiev, Ukraine	2,619,900	• Kiev, the capital and largest city of the Ukraine, was the capital of Kievan Rus, the first East Slavic state, during the late 800s.
Africa		
Algiers, Algeria	1,650,300	• Algiers lies along the Mediterranean Sea, and its waterfront is lined with white buildings.
Cairo, Egypt	7,594,800	• The old sections of Cairo contain numerous bazaars and more than 300 mosques, many of which exemplify outstanding Islamic architecture.
Nairobi, Kenya	2,391,600	• Within the city of Nairobi is a national park where lions, zebras, and other African wildlife roam the open land.
Cape Town, South Africa	2,639,500	• Cape Town is a popular vacation spot because of its sandy beach and sunny climate.
Southwest Asia		
Jerusalem, Israel	671,700	• Jerusalem is a holy city of three religions—Judaism, Christianity, and Islam.
Beirut, Lebanon	1,135,800	• Beirut was a leading cultural and commercial center of Southwest Asia until its economy was crippled by a civil war between Christians and Muslims that lasted from 1975 to 1991.
Riyadh, Saudi Arabia	3,533,500	• Riyadh is the headquarters of the oil industry in Saudi Arabia, which makes it an international business center.
Istanbul, Turkey	9,018,500	• Istanbul is the only major city located on two continents—Asia and Europe. It has been the capital of three historic empires—the Roman, Byzantine, and Ottoman empires.
South Asia		
Mumbai, India	12,916,600	• Mumbai, India's largest city, is located on an island and is connected to the mainland by bridges.
Islamabad, Pakistan	571,700	• Islamabad, the capital of Pakistan, is a planned city that was built during the 1960s and has a blend of modern and traditional Islamic architecture.
East Asia		
Beijing, China	6,995,500	• Beijing, the capital of China, contains the Forbidden City, where former Chinese emperors lived.
Tokyo, Japan	8,021,500	• Tokyo, the capital of Japan, has the most neon signs of any city in the world.
Southeast Asia, Oceania, and Antarctica		
Sydney, Australia	3,985,800	• Sydney, the oldest and largest city in Australia, was founded as a prison colony in 1788.
Manila, Philippines	10,032,900	• Manila was nicknamed the "Pearl of the Orient" because of its beautiful setting on a mountain-lined bay and its architectural treasures.
Bangkok, Thailand	6,416,200	• Bangkok is famous for its magnificent palaces and temples, including the Grand Palace and the Temple of the Emerald Buddha.
Ho Chi Minh City, Vietnam	3,341,900	• Ho Chi Minh City, formerly called Saigon, reflects its country's history of occupation in its Chinese, French-colonial, and modern buildings.

* inside political border of city

Government Systems

System	Definition	Example
Aristocracy/ Monarchy	• Power is in the hands of a hereditary ruling class or nobility.	• present-day Saudi Arabia
Autocracy	• A single person rules with unlimited power.	• Germany in the 1930s and 1940s under Adolf Hitler
Democracy/ Republic	• Citizens hold political power either directly or through representatives.	• direct democracy: ancient Athens; representative democracy: present-day United States
Federal	• Powers are divided among the national government and state governments.	• present-day United States
Feudalism	• A king allows nobles to use his land in exchange for their loyalty and military service.	• Medieval Europe
Military state	• Military leaders rule, supported by the power of the armed forces.	• Argentina between 1955 and 1983
Oligarchy	• a few persons or a small group rule	• most ancient Greek city-states
Parliamentary	• Legislative and executive functions are combined in a legislature called a parliament.	• present-day United Kingdom
Theocracy	• Religious leaders control the government, relying on religious law and consultation with religious scholars.	• present-day Iran
Totalitarianism	• The government controls every aspect of public and private life.	• Soviet Union under Joseph Stalin

Economic Systems

System	Definition	Example
Command	• The production of goods and services is determined by a central government.	• former Soviet Union
Communism	• All means of production—land, mines, factories, railroads, and businesses—are owned by the people. Private property does not exist.	• former Soviet Union
Free Enterprise	• Businesses are privately owned and operate competitively for profit with minimal government interference.	• present-day United States
Manorialism	• A lord gives serfs land, shelter, and protection in exchange for work, and almost everything needed for daily life is produced on the manor, or lord's estate.	• Medieval Europe
Mixed	• A combination of command and market economies is designed to provide goods and services so that all people will benefit.	• present-day Israel
Socialism	• The means of production are owned by the public and operate for the welfare of all.	• Present-day countries, including Denmark and Sweden
Traditional	• Goods and services are exchanged without the use of money.	• many ancient civilizations and tribal societies

World Religions

	Buddhism	Christianity	Hinduism	Islam	Judaism	Confucianism
Followers Worldwide*	338 million	1.9 billion	764 million	1 billion	13.4 million	not available
Name of Deity	The Buddha did not teach a personal deity.	God	Three main Gods: Brahma, Vishnu, Shiva	God (Allah)	God (Yahweh)	Confucius (viewed by many as a god)
Founder	The Buddha	Jesus Christ	No one founder	Muhammad	Abraham	Confucius
Holy Book	No one book—sacred texts, including the *Perfection of Wisdom Sutra*	Bible	No one book—sacred texts, including the Vedas, the Puranas	Qur'an	Hebrew Bible, including the Torah	the *Analects*, the Five Classics
Leadership	Buddhist monks and nuns	Clergy (priests/ministers)	Guru, Holy Man, Brahmin priest	No clergy	Rabbis	No Clergy
Basic Beliefs	• Persons achieve complete peace and happiness, known as nirvana, by eliminating their attachment to worldly things. • Nirvana is reached by following the Noble Eightfold Path: Right views; Right aspirations; Right speech; Right conduct; Right livelihood; Right endeavor; Right mindfulness; Right meditation.	• There is only one God, who watches over and cares for his people. • Jesus Christ was the son of God. He died to save humanity from sin. His death and resurrection made eternal life possible for others.	• The soul never dies, but is continually reborn. • Persons achieve happiness and enlightenment after they free themselves from their earthly desires. • Freedom from earthly desires comes from a lifetime of worship, knowledge, and virtuous acts.	• Persons achieve salvation by following the Five Pillars of Islam and living a just life. These pillars are: faith; almsgiving, or charity to the poor; fasting, which Muslims perform during Ramadan; pilgrimage (to Mecca); and prayer.	• There is only one God, who watches over and cares for his people. • God loves and protects his people, but also holds people accountable for their sins and shortcomings. • Persons serve God by studying the Torah and living by its teachings.	• Social order, harmony, and good government should be based on strong family relationships. • Respect for parents and elders is important to a well-ordered society. • Education is important both to the welfare of the individual and to society.

* estimated 1994 figures

Major Explorations

Area Explored	Dates	Explorer(s)	Nationality
Newfoundland	about 1000	Leif Ericson	Norse
West Indies, South and Central America	1492–1502	Christopher Columbus	Italian
Newfoundland	1497	John and Sebastian Cabot	Italian
Cape of Good Hope, Africa; India	1497–1498	Vasco da Gama	Portuguese
East and north coast of South America	1497–1499	Vespucci	Italian
Brazil	1500	Pedro Alvarez Cabral	Portuguese
Panama, Pacific Ocean	1513	Vasco Nunez de Balboa	Spanish
Florida, Yucatán Peninsula	1513	Juan Ponce de Leon	Spanish
Mexico	1519	Hernando Cortés	Spanish
Straits of Magellan, Tierra del Fuego	1519–1520	Ferdinand Magellan	Portuguese
New York harbor	1524	Giovanni da Verrazano	Italian
Texas	1528	Cabeza de Vaca	Spanish
Peru	1532	Francisco Pizarro	Spanish
Canada, Gulf of St. Lawrence	1534	Jacques Cartier	French
Buenos Aires	1536	Pedro de Mendoza	Spanish
Mississippi River, near Memphis	1539–1541	Hernando de Soto	Spanish
Southwestern United States	1540	Francisco de Coronado	Spanish
Colorado River	1540	Hernando Alarcon	Spanish
Colorado, Grand Canyon	1540	Garcia de Lopez Cardenas	Spanish
Amazon River	1541	Francisco de Orellana	Spanish
Western Mexico, San Diego harbor	1542	Juan Rodriguez Cabrillo	Portuguese
California coast	1577–1580	Sir Francis Drake	English
Orinoco river	1595	Sir Walter Raleigh	English
Canadian interior, Lake Champlain	1603–1609	Samuel de Champlain	French
Hudson River, Hudson Bay	1609–1610	Henry Hudson	English
Mississippi River, south to Arkansas	1673	Jacques Marquette, Louis Joliet	French
Mississippi River, south to Gulf of Mexico	1682	Robert Cavelier, sieur de La Salle	French
Bering Strait and Alaska	1727–1729	Vitus Bering	Danish
Northwestern Canada	1789	Sir Alexander Mackenzie	Canadian
Missouri River, Rocky Mountains, Columbia River	1804–1805	Meriwether Lewis, William Clark	American
Arabia, East Africa, Lake Tanganyika	1853–1858	Sir Richard Burton	English
Upper course of Zambezi River, Victoria Falls, Lake Ngami	1849–1873	David Livingstone	Scottish
Congo River	1874–1889	Sir Henry Stanley	Welsh
South Pacific	1768–1775	James Cook	English
Tasmania	1642	Abel Janszoon	Dutch
China, Southeast Asia, India	1770s–1790s	Marco Polo	Venetian
North Pole	1909	Robert E. Peary, Matthew Henson	American
South Pole	1911	Roald Amundsen	Norwegian
Moon	1969	Neil Armstrong, Edwin Aldrin	American
Mars	1975	Space probes Viking 1 and 2	American

Major Disasters

Disaster	Date	Description
Disease		
bubonic plague	mid-1300s	• The plague spread to Europe from Central Asia and killed an estimated 25 million Europeans—about one-fourth of the population.
Flu epidemic	1918–1919	• An outbreak of flu spread around the world and killed about 30 million people.
AIDS epidemic	1980s–2000s	• By 2000, AIDS had killed about 19 million people worldwide.
Flood		
Huang He	1887	• This flood of the Huang He in China killed more than a million people.
Chang Jiang	1931	• The Chang Jiang flooded more than 35,000 square miles of land, causing many thousands of deaths.
Asteroid		
Chicxulub event	about 65 million years ago	• An asteroid about ten miles across hit near Chicxulub on the Yucatan Peninsula of Mexico. It dug a crater 110 miles across and about 12 miles deep under the Caribbean Sea. The hit changed the environment so drastically—causing fires, darkened skies, acid rain, and a greenhouse effect— that 50 to 70 percent of all living species on earth were wiped out.
Tunguska event	June 30, 1908	• An explosion—perhaps caused by an asteroid hit—occurred over the Tunguska region of Siberia. The fireball burned 800,000 acres of forest.
Volcanic eruption		
Mount Tambora	1815	• The eruption of this volcano in Indonesia killed 92,000 people. The energy it released was 6 million times more than that of an atomic bomb.
Krakatoa	1883	• The eruption of this Indonesian volcano sent volcanic ash 50 miles into the air. It collapsed into the sea and triggered a series of deadly tsunamis that swept the coasts of Java and Sumatra, killing more than 36,000 people.
Earthquake		
Northern Egypt	1201	• This earthquake killed about 1,100,000 people.
New Madrid, Missouri	1811–1812	• A series of earthquakes that measured up to 8.8 on the Richter scale and temporarily caused the Mississippi River to flow backward.
Tornado		
Missouri, Illinois, Indiana	1925	• One of the most deadly tornadoes in history cut a path about 220 miles long and up to a mile wide and traveled about 60 miles an hour. It killed 689 people
Drought		
Dust Bowl	1930s	• A ten-year drought, plus unwise farming practices, contributed to the mile-high dust storms that blew away hundreds of millions of tons of topsoil in the southwestern Great Plains. Nearly three million people abandoned their farms in the area that became known as the Dust Bowl.
Famine		
Chinese Famine	1958–1960	• An estimated 20 million people died of starvation when the Chinese government forced farmers onto communes trying to increase agricultural output.
Irish Potato Famine	1845–1849	• A disease called blight destroyed potato crops, resulting in the deaths of over one million people.
Cyclone and Tsunami		
Bangladesh	1970	• A cyclone and tsunami killed more than 300,000 people and left hundreds of thousands homeless.
Blizzard		
East Coast, United States	1888	• On March 11–14, a blizzard dropped up to 5 feet of snow on the East Coast and killed 400 people.

Major Modifications of the Environment

Three Gorges Dam
Scheduled to be completed in 2009, the Three Gorges Dam on the Chang Jiang (Yangtze River) in China will be the world's biggest dam. It will create a reservoir nearly 400 miles long and put hundreds of square miles of land under water. Between one and two million people will be forced to move.
Aswan High Dam
Completed in 1970, this dam created Lake Nasser, which is nearly 300 miles long. The dam has helped Egypt avoid droughts and floods and has increased farmable land by 50 percent. But the dam also has decreased the fertility of the soil because the Nile no longer deposits its rich silt on the farmland.
Damming of the Colorado River
More than 20 dams have been constructed on the river and its tributaries to provide hydroelectric power, irrigation, and drinking water to much of the Southwest. As a result, the river no longer flows into the Gulf of California as it formerly did. It trickles away near the towns of Tijuana and Mexicali in Mexico.
Polders of the Netherlands
More than 40 percent of the land that makes up the Netherlands was once covered by the sea, lakes, or swamps. The Dutch reclaimed the land by building dikes and draining the water to create polders.
Deforestation in the United States and in the Amazon Region
The present-day United States held about one billion acres of wild forests. By the end of the 20th century, 95 percent of those forests had been cut down. The Amazon rain forest covers 2.5 million square miles, and loses about 20,000 square miles a year.
Shrinkage of the Aral Sea
The Aral Sea was once the world's fourth largest lake. But extensive irrigation projects have diverted so much water away from this Central Asian saltwater lake that it has lost about 80 percent of its water volume. Scientists predict the Aral Sea may disappear entirely by 2010.
Urbanization of the U.S. Atlantic Coast
The growth of cities and suburbs along the Atlantic Coast of the United States has completely altered the natural landscape across a huge area. Today, about 500 miles of highly urbanized areas stretch from Boston in the north to Washington, D.C., in the south. This region covers over 50,000 square miles.
Ozone Depletion over Antarctica
In 1974, scientists became aware that certain air pollutants were capable of breaking down the ozone layer above the earth, which shields the earth's surface from intense radiation from the sun. They discovered an "ozone hole" above Antarctica, which has grown to double the size of Antarctica.
Nuclear Contamination of Bikini Atoll
After World War II, the U.S. government tested atomic weapons on Bikini Atoll in the Marshall Islands of the central Pacific. These islands became contaminated with radiation and are still not suitable for human life.
Destruction of Kuwait's Oil Fields
Near the end of the Persian Gulf War in 1991, Iraq blew up a series of tankers and oil storage terminals in Kuwait and on islands off its coast. Over 600 oil well fires spewed black smoke into the air. More than 240 million gallons of crude oil were spilled, the largest oil spill on record.

Major Works of World Literature

Title and Date	Author	Culture	Description
A Doll's House **(1879)**	Henrik Ibsen	Norwegian	• Play about a woman who feels treated like a doll by her husband
Adventures of Huckleberry Finn **(1884)**	Mark Twain	American	• Novel about a young boy who helps a runaway slave
Aeneid **(between 30–19 B.C.)**	Virgil	Roman	• Epic poem about the Trojan hero Aeneas
Analects **(about 400 B.C.)**	followers of Confucius	Chinese	• Teachings of Confucius
The Thousand and One Nights **(about 1500)**	Unknown	Arabic	• Collection of folk tales from Arabia, Egypt, India, Persia, and other countries
Beowulf **(700s)**	Unknown	English	• Epic poem about a mighty warrior who fights a monster named Grendel
Book of the Dead **(1500s B.C.)**	Unknown	Egyptian	• Hymns, prayers, and magic spells intended to guide the soul in the afterlife
Brothers Karamozov **(1879–1880)**	Fyodor Dostoevsky	Russian	• Novel about the effects of the murder of a father on each of his four sons
Candide	Voltaire	French	• Novel about the nature of good and evil
Canterbury Tales **(about 1386–1400)**	Geoffrey Chaucer	English	• Verse tales told by pilgrims on their way to Canterbury
Divine Comedy **(about 1308–1321)**	Dante Alighieri	Italian	• Epic poem about life after death
Don Quixote **(1605–1615)**	Miguel de Cervantes	Spanish	• Novel about a Spanish landowner who wishes to live like the knights of old
Epic of Gilgamesh **(before 2000 B.C.)**	unknown	Mesopotamian	• Epic poem about a Sumerian king who searches for the secret of immortality
Faust **(1808, 1832)**	Johann Wolfgang von Goethe	German	• Verse drama about a magician who sells his soul to the devil
Hebrew Bible (after about 1000 B.C.)	unknown	Hebrew	• Sacred book of Judaism
Iliad **(700s B.C.)**	Homer	Greek	• Epic poem about the Trojan War
King Lear **(1608)**	William Shakespeare	English	• Drama about an aged British king and his daughters
Leaves of Grass **(1855–1882)**	Walt Whitman	American	• Collection of poems that celebrate American life
Mahabharata **(about 500 B.C.)**	unknown	Indian	• Epic poem about a great war between two sets of cousins
Odyssey **(700s B.C.)**	Homer	Greek	• Epic poem about the journey home of an Ithacan king, Odysseus, after the Trojan War
One Hundred Years of Solitude **(1967)**	Gabriel García Márquez	Colombian	• Novel about several generations of a Latin American family, written in a style called magic realism
Panchatantra **(200s B.C.?)**	unknown	Indian	• Collection of fables
Paradise Lost **(1667–1674)**	John Milton	English	• Epic poem based on the Biblical story of creation/
Popol Vuh **(1500s)**	unknown	Mayan	• Story of creation
Qu'ran (A.D. 610–632)	unknown	Muslim	• Sacred book of Islam
Rig Veda **(about 1400 B.C.)**	unknown	Indian	• Oldest of the four Vedas, which are sacred books of Hinduism
Tale of Genji **(1000s?)**	Murasaki Shikibu	Japanese	• Novel about Japanese court life
Tao Te Ching, **also spelled** ***Dao de Ching*** **(200s–100s B.C.)**	Laozi	Chinese	• Teachings of Taoism, also called Daoism
The Sound and the Fury **(1929)**	William Faulkner	American	• Novel about the breakup of an old Southern family
Things Fall Apart **(1958)**	Chinua Achebe	Nigerian	• Novel about the effects of British colonialism on the Igbo, also spelled Ibo
Ulysses **(1922)**	James Joyce	Irish	• Novel that draws parallels between the main character and the hero of the Greek epic *The Odyssey*
War and Peace **(1869)**	Leo Tolstoy	Russian	• Novel about Napoleon's invasion of Russia in 1812

Cultures Around the World

United States and Canada

- Distinctive American forms of music includes jazz, blues, gospel, and rock 'n' roll, which have African-American origins. Country and bluegrass music developed among Southern whites whose ancestors came from the British Isles.
- The skyscraper is an American creation that has influenced urban architecture throughout the world.
- Americans have strongly influenced the artistic development of motion pictures.
- Distinctive Canadian visual arts include the realistic soapstone and bone carvings of the Inuit and the elaborately decorated totem poles of the First Nations people of the West Coast.

Latin America

- Mexico is known for its public art, especially murals that are painted on the walls of public buildings depicting the history of the country. These murals blend European and Native American art styles.
- Two forms of music—calypso and reggae—originated in the Caribbean region. Calypso combines musical elements from Africa, Spain, and the United States. Reggae has its roots in African, Caribbean, and American music.
- Throughout South America, street musicians playing drums, guitars, marimbas, maracas, and flutes create music that combines Indian, African, and European elements. An example of such music is the tango of Argentina.
- Capoeira is a martial art and dance that developed in Brazil and has African roots. The samba is another Brazilian dance with African influences.

Europe

- Western civilization has its roots in Greece and Rome, where many treasures of classical architecture and sculpture can be found. Europe is also known for its Renaissance painting and sculpture, as well as for the works of such modern artists as Pablo Picasso of Spain.
- Germany and Austria are especially known for their contributions to classical music. Their greatest composers include Wolfgang Amadeus Mozart of Austria and Ludwig van Beethoven of Germany.

Russia and the Republics

- Russia is internationally famous for its ballet and has produced such magnificent dancers as Rudolf Nureyev and Mikhail Baryshnikov.
- Well-known Russian composers of operas, ballet scores, and instrumental music include Modest Mussorgsky, Nikolai Rimsky-Korsakov, Peter Ilich Tchaikovsky, Alexander Borodin, Sergei Rachmaninoff, and Igor Stravinsky.
- In architecture, Russia is known for its Byzantine churches with distinctive onion-shaped domes and stylized religious paintings called icons.

Africa

- North Africa is known for its Islamic architecture, especially mosques topped with domes and towers called minarets.
- Africa south of the Sahara is noted for its sculpture, especially masks. Each ethnic group has developed its own form and style of sculpture. For example, the Fang of Central Africa are famous for masks that are painted white with facial features outlined in black. The simple, dramatic forms of African sculpture influenced many modern Western artists.
- African music has had a great influence on Western music. Much traditional African music features complex rhythms and flattened notes. Call-and-response singing, in which a lead singer sings a phrase and a group responds by repeating the phrase or singing a refrain, is common. In African dances, each part of the dancer's body may move to a different rhythm.

Southwest Asia
• Southwest Asia is especially known for its Islamic architecture, especially domed mosques with minarets. • Islamic artists developed a style of decoration called *arabesque,* which consists of patterns of winding stems with leaves. Sophisticated geometric patterns are also characteristic of Islamic art.
South Asia
• Islamic architecture spread to South Asia, and its influence can be seen in the Taj Mahal at Agra, India, considered one of the world's most beautiful buildings. Indian architecture and art have also been influence by Buddhism and Hinduism • In Indian music, the notes of the scale are arranged in patterns called ragas. A performer plays a raga and improvises on it, using a stringed instrument such as the sitar or vina. • *Qawwali,* a form of devotional music performed by Muslims known as Sufis, is famous in South Asia. • The Maldives has a popular tradition of music and dance based on drumming, called *bodu beru.* Dancers swing and sway to the drumbeat with increasing intensity.
East Asia
• In Japan, noh plays, which deal with subjects drawn from history and legend and are performed by actors wearing masks, are a traditional form of drama. Another form is kabuki plays, which feature lively scenery, an exaggerated acting style, and vivid costumes. • In art, the Japanese are known for their wood-block prints, long picture scrolls, and ink paintings. Japanese Buddhist temples feature tile roofs with edges that extend out and curve upward. • A Chinese form of drama is the Beijing opera, which includes music, dancing, and acrobatics. • Traditional Chinese music does not have harmony, and the basic scale has five notes.
Southeast Asia and Oceania
• Indonesia is famous for its traditional dances and shadow puppet dramas. Javanese dances feature slow, intricate movements that have symbolic meaning. Balinese dances, in contrast, are more dramatic. Indonesian shadow puppet plays typically last all night. An orchestra called a *gamelan,* which makes great use of gongs, accompanies both dances and puppet plays. • The Sydney Opera House in Australia, with its sail-like roofs, is considered one of the finest works of 20th-century architecture. • The Maori of New Zealand are known for their intricate woodcarvings.

Geographic Terms

absolute location the exact place on earth where a geographic feature is found.
acculturation the cultural change that occurs when individuals in a society accept or adopt an innovation.
acid rain rainwater that is chemically changed by air pollution in the atmosphere.
alluvial plain land that is rich farmland, composed of clay, silt, sand, or gravel deposited by running water.
archipelago a set of closely grouped islands.
assimilation a process whereby a minority group gradually gives up its own culture and adopts the culture of a majority group.
atmosphere the layers of gases immediately surrounding the earth.
atoll a ring-like coral island or string of small islands surrounding a lagoon.

biodiversity the variety of organisms within an ecosystem.
biome a regional ecosystem.
biosphere all the parts of the earth where plants and animals live, including the atmosphere, the lithosphere, and the hydrosphere.

carrying capacity the number of organisms a piece of land can support without negative effects.
cerrado a savanna that has flat terrain and moderate rainfall, which make it suitable for farming.
chaparral the term, in some locations, for a biome of drought-resistant trees.
chemical weathering a process that changes rock into a new substance through interactions among elements in the air or water and the minerals in the rock.
chernozem black topsoil, one of the world's most fertile soils.
climate the typical weather conditions at a particular location as observed over time.
commodity an agricultural or mining product that can be sold.
confederation a political union.
coniferous another word for needle-leaf trees.
conservation the management, protection, and wise use of natural resources.
continent a landmass above water on the earth.
continental drift the theory that the earth was once a supercontinent that divided and slowly drifted apart over millions of years.
continentality a region's distance from the moderating influence of the sea.
continental shelf the earth's surface from the edge of a continent to the deep part of the ocean.
convection the transfer of heat in the atmosphere by upward motion of the air.
core the solid metallic center of the earth, made up of iron and nickel under tremendous pressure.
crust the thin layer of rock on the surface of the earth.
cultural crossroad a place where various cultures cross paths.
cultural hearth the heartland or place of origin of a major culture; a site of innovation from which basic ideas, materials, and technology diffuse to other cultures.
culture the total of knowledge, attitudes, and behaviors shared by and passed on by members of a group.

cyclone a violent storm with fierce winds and heavy rain; the most extreme weather pattern of South Asia.
deciduous shedding leaves at the end of a growing season. It is a characteristic of broadleaf trees, such as maple, oak, birch, and cottonwood.
deforestation the cutting down and clearing away of trees and forests.
delta a fan-like landform made of deposited sediment, left by a river that slows as it enters the ocean.
desalinization the removal of salt from ocean water.
desertification an expansion of dry conditions to moist areas that are next to deserts.
diffusion the spread of ideas, inventions, or patterns of behavior to different societies.
diversify to increase the variety of products in a country's economy; to promote manufacturing and other industries in order to achieve growth and stability.
drainage basin an area drained by a major river and its tributaries.
drought a long period without rain or with minimal rainfall.

ecosystem an interdependent community of plants and animals.
equator the imaginary line that encircles the globe, dividing the earth into northern and southern halves.
equinox each of the two days in a year on which day and night are equal in length; marks the beginning of spring and autumn.
erosion the result of weathering on matter, created by the action of wind, water, ice, or gravity.
escarpment a steep slope with a nearly flat plateau on top.
estuary a broadened seaward end of a river, where the river's currents meet the ocean's tides.

fault a fracture in the earth's crust.
fertility rate the average number of children a woman of childbearing years would have in her lifetime, if she had children at the current rate for her country.
fjord a long, narrow, deep inlet of the sea between steep slopes.

Geographic Information System (GIS) technology that uses digital map information to create a databank. Different "data layers" can be combined to produce specialized maps. GIS allows geographers to analyze different aspects of a specific place to solve problems.
glaciation the changing of landforms by slowly moving glaciers.
global economy the merging of regional economies in which nations become dependent on each other for goods and services.
global warming a worldwide rise in temperature caused by the buildup of carbon dioxide in the atmosphere, which prevents heat from escaping into space.
greenhouse effect the trapping of solar energy by a layer of gases that are released by the burning of coal and petroleum, causing global temperature to increase.
Gross Domestic Product (GDP) the value of only those goods and services that are produced within a country in a period of time.
Gross National Product (GNP) the total value of all goods and services produced by a country in a period of time, whether they are produced within or outside the country.
ground water the water held under the earth's surface, often in and around the pores of rock.

hemisphere each half of the globe.
humus organic material in soil.
hydrologic cycle the continuous circulation of water among the atmosphere, the oceans, and the earth.
hydrosphere the waters comprising the earth's surface, including oceans, seas, rivers, lakes, and vapor in the atmosphere.

industrialization the growth of industry in a country or a society.
infant mortality rate the number of deaths among infants under age one as measured per thousand live births.
infrastructure the basic support systems needed to keep an economy going, including power, communications, transportation, water, sanitation, and education systems.

landfill a method of solid waste disposal in which refuse is buried between layers of dirt.
landform a naturally formed feature on the surface of the earth.
landlocked having no outlet to the sea.
latitude a set of imaginary lines that run parallel to the equator and that are used in locating places north or south. The equator is labeled the zero-degree line for latitude.
lithosphere the solid rock portion of the earth's surface.
loess wind-blown silt and clay sediment that produces very fertile soil.
longitude a set of imaginary lines that go around the earth over the poles, dividing it east and west. The prime meridian is labeled the zero-degree line for longitude.

magma the molten rock created when the mantle melts the underside of the earth's crust.
mantle a soft layer about 1,800 miles thick of molten rock, which floats on the earth's core.
mechanical weathering natural processes that break rock into smaller pieces.
megalopolis a region in which several large cities and surrounding areas grow together.
metropolitan area a functional area including a city and its surrounding suburbs and exurbs, linked economically.
mistral a cold, dry wind from the north.
monsoon a seasonal wind, especially in South Asia.
moraine a ridge or hill of rock carried and finally deposited by a glacier.
mortality rate the number of deaths per thousand.

nationalism the belief that people should be loyal to their nation, the people with whom they share land, culture, and history.
nation-state the name of a territory when a nation and a state occupy the same territory.
natural resource a material on or in the earth, such as a tree, fish, or coal, that has economic value.
oasis a place in a desert where water from an aquifer has reached the surface; it supports vegetation and wildlife.
ozone a chemical created when the products from burning fossil fuels react with sunlight; a form of oxygen.

pampas a vast area of grassland and rich soil in south-central South America.
pandemic a disease affecting a large population over a wide geographic area.
per capita income the average amount of money earned by each person in a political unit.
permafrost permanently frozen ground.
population density the average number of people who live in a measurable area, reached by dividing the number of inhabitants in an area by the amount of land they occupy.
population pyramid a graphic device that shows the gender and age distribution of a population.
postindustrial economy an economic phase in which manufacturing no longer plays a dominant role.
precipitation falling water droplets in the form of rain, sleet, snow, or hail.
prevailing westerlies winds that blow from west to east.
prime meridian the imaginary line at zero meridian that is used to measure longitude east to west and that divides the earth's east and west halves. It is also called the Greenwich Meridian because it passes through Greenwich, England.

pull factor a factor that draws or attracts people to another location.
push factor a factor that causes people to leave their homeland and migrate to another region.

rain forest a forest region located in the tropical zone, having a heavy concentration of different species of broadleaf trees.
rain shadow the land on the leeward side of hills or mountains that gets little rain from the descending dry air.
rate of natural increase the rate at which a population is growing, found by subtracting the mortality rate from the birthrate. It is also called the population growth rate.
recession an extended period of decline in general business activity.
relative location the description of a place in relation to other places around it.
relief the difference in elevation of a landform from the lowest point to the highest point.
Richter scale a way to measure information collected by seismographs to determine the relative strength of an earthquake.
rift valley a long, thin valley created by the moving apart of the continental plates. The Great Rift Valley in East Africa extends over 4,000 miles from Jordan in Southwest Asia to Mozambique in southern Africa.
runoff rainfall that is not absorbed by soil and that runs into streams.
savanna flat, grassy, mostly treeless plain in the tropical grassland region.
sectionalism when people place their loyalty to their region, or section, above loyalty to the nation.
sediment small pieces of rock produced by weathering.
seismograph a device that measures the size of the waves created by an earthquake.
service industry any kind of economic activity that produces a service rather than a product.
silt loose sedimentary material consisting of very small rock particles, carried by rivers and very fertile.
sirocco a hot, steady south wind that blows from North Africa across the Mediterranean Sea into southern Europe, mostly in spring.
smart growth the efficient use and conservation of land and other resources.
solar system the sun and nine known planets, as well as other celestial bodies that orbit the sun.
solstice either of two times of year when the sun's rays shine directly overhead at noon at the farthest points north or south, and that mark the beginning of summer and winter. In the Northern Hemisphere, the summer solstice is the longest day and the winter solstice is the shortest.
stateless nation a nation of people who do not have a territory to legally occupy, such as the Palestinians, the Kurds, and the Basques.
stateless society one in which people use lineages, or families whose members are descended from a common ancestry, to govern themselves.
steppe the term used for the temperate grassland region in the Northern Hemisphere.
storm surge high water level brought by a cyclone that swamps low-lying areas.
strategic commodity a resource so important that nations will go to war to ensure its steady supply.
subcontinent a landmass that is like a continent, only smaller, such as South Asia, which is called the Indian subcontinent.
subsistence activity an activity in which a family produces only the food, clothing, and shelter they themselves need.
sustainable community a community where residents can live and work in harmony with the environment.
taiga a nearly continuous belt of evergreen coniferous forests across the Northern Hemisphere, in North America and Eurasia.
tectonic plate an enormous moving shelf that forms the earth's crust.
terraced farming an ancient technique for growing crops on hillsides or mountain slopes, using step-like horizontal fields cut into the slopes.
topographic map a general reference map that shows natural and man-made features on the earth.
topography the combined characteristics of landforms and their distribution in a region.
tsunami a giant ocean wave, caused by an underwater earthquake or volcanic eruption, with great destructive power.
tundra the flat treeless lands forming a ring around the Arctic Ocean; the climate region of the Arctic Ocean.
typhoon a tropical storm, like a hurricane, that occurs in the western Pacific.

upland an area of hills or very low mountains that may also contain mesas and high plateaus.
urbanization the dramatic rise in the number of cities and the changes in lifestyle that result.
urban sprawl poorly planned development that spreads a city's population over a wider and wider geographic area.

wadi a riverbed that remains dry except during the rainy seasons.
water table the level at which rock is saturated.
weather the condition of the atmosphere at a particular location and time.
weathering physical and chemical processes that change the characteristics of rock on or near the earth's surface, occurring

Name ______________________________ Date ______________

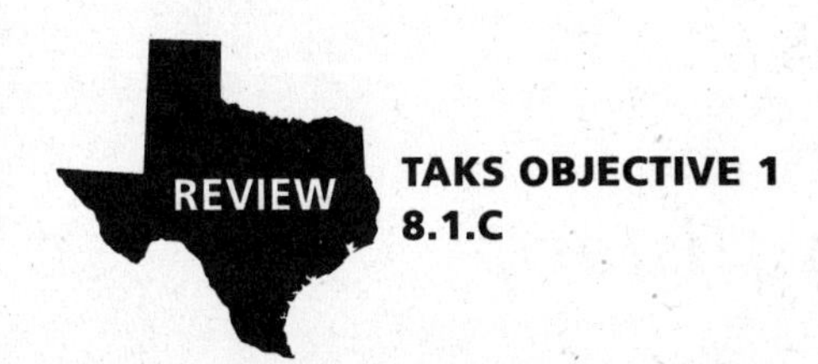

TAKS OBJECTIVE 1
8.1.C

Key Dates in American History

Learning Objective Explain the significance of the following dates: 1776, 1787, and 1861–1865. This time line highlights the significance of the key dates you need to remember. Some tips for remembering dates are given below the time line. Review the time line and the tips to answer the questions on the next page.

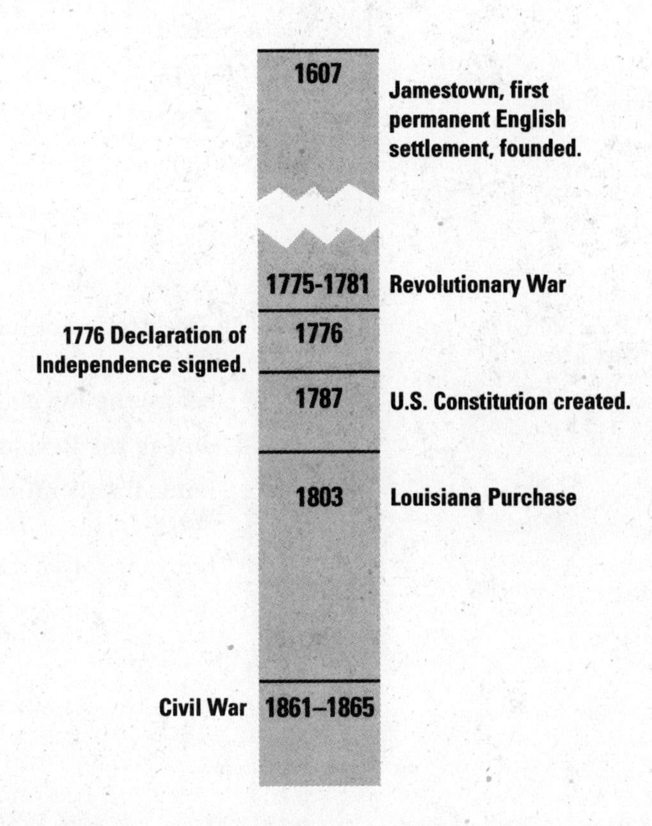

Ways to Remember Dates

- 1776 Make up a rhyme, even if it is a silly one, to remember the date:
  Independence was the fix in 1776.
- 1787 Use reasoning. You know that the colonies declared independence in 1776. Remember that the U.S. Constitution was created about ten years after independence was declared.
- 1861–1865 A range in dates often indicates a war. Remember that the Civil War occurred almost 100 years after the Declaration of Independence was signed. Try this rhyme to help yourself remember:
  The Civil War had just begun in 1861. The end did arrive in 1865.

Name ______________________ Date ______________

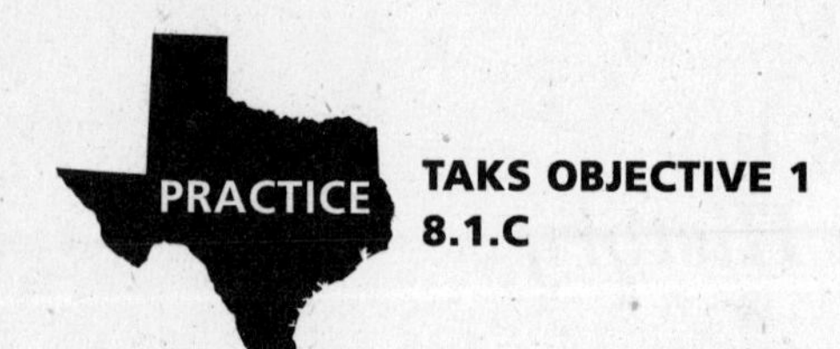

TAKS OBJECTIVE 1
8.1.C

Key Dates in American History

Directions: Read the following questions and choose the best answer from among the four alternatives.

1 Which of the following documents was signed in 1776?

A U.S. Constitution

B Declaration of Independence

C Mayflower Compact

D Bill of Rights

2 The dates of the Civil War are—

F 1754–1763

G 1775–1781

H 1848–1849

J 1861–1865

3 The U.S. Constitution was created in—

A 1620

B 1775

C 1787

D 1803

4 The Declaration of Independence was signed—

F before the Revolutionary War

G during the Revolutionary War

H immediately after the Revolutionary War

J ten years after the Revolutionary War

Name ______________________ Date ____________

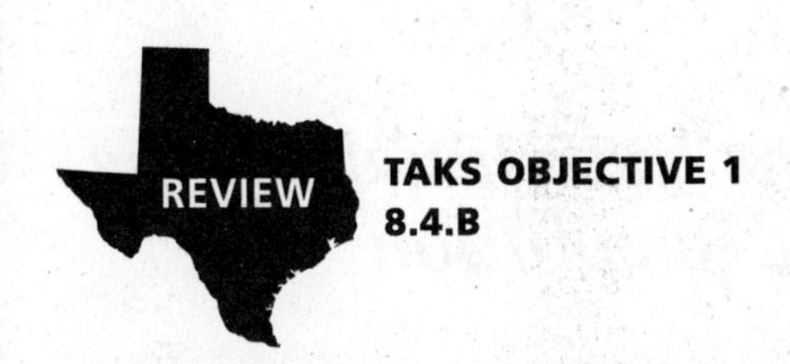

TAKS OBJECTIVE 1
8.4.B

Significant Individuals of the American Revolution

Learning Objective Explain the roles played by significant individuals during the American Revolution, including Thomas Jefferson and George Washington.

These cluster diagrams outline the roles played by Thomas Jefferson and George Washington during the American Revolution. Memorize these facts about these two important American leaders to answer the questions on the following page.

Roles during Revolutionary War

Thomas Jefferson
- Delegate to Continental Congress
- Wrote Declaration of Independence

George Washington
- Delegate to Continental Congress
- Commanding general of Continental Army
- Formed, trained, and directed the Continental Army
- Helped unite Americans and inspire soldiers
- Developed strategy that won the war—wear the British down and never give-up

Name ______________________________ Date ______________

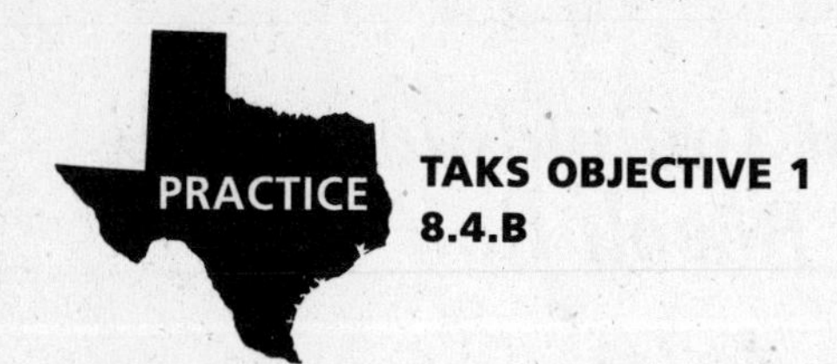

TAKS OBJECTIVE 1
8.4.B

Significant Individuals of the American Revolution

Directions: Read the following questions and choose the best answer from among the four alternatives.

1 Thomas Jefferson's most important contribution to the American Revolution was writing—

A *Common Sense*

B the *Declaration of Independence*

C the *American Crisis*

D the *Treaty of Paris*

2 During the American Revolution, George Washington served as—

F commanding general of the Continental Army

G president of the United States

H commanding general of the Loyalists

J the ambassador to Great Britain

3 Which of the following does not accurately describe Washington's role in the American Revolution?

A His popularity helped unite Americans in support of the war.

B He developed the winning strategy of wearing the British down.

C He was ultimately responsible for recruiting, training, and directing the Continental Army.

D He won every battle that he fought against the British.

4 Which of the following positions did Thomas Jefferson hold during the American Revolution?

F Delegate to the Constitutional Congress

G President of the United States

H Commanding general of the Confederate Army

J Captain of the Continental Navy

Name ______________________________ Date ______________

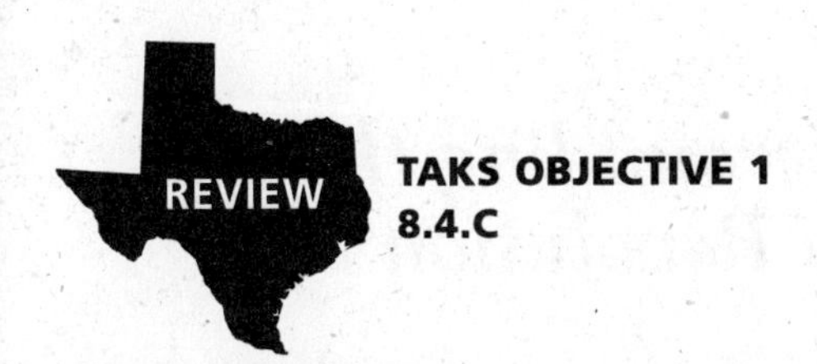

TAKS OBJECTIVE 1
8.4.C

Issues Surrounding the American Revolution

Learning Objective Explain the issues surrounding the American Revolution, including declaring independence and writing the Articles of Confederation. The following outlines summarize the key issues that prompted the colonists to declare independence and to write the Articles of Confederation. Review these key issues to answer the questions on the following page.

Issues Surrounding the Declaration of Independence	Issues Surrounding the Articles of Confederation
1. Control of the colonies • Until the French and Indian War, Britain allowed the colonies to develop and operate independently. After the war, Britain reversed its policy and tried to gain more control so that it could uniformly govern the colonies and territories that it gained in the war. • Britain passed new laws and restrictions. To enforce these laws, the British sent troops and required the colonists to house and supply these troops.	**1. Areas of agreement among colonists** • Americans realized they needed to unite to win the war against the British. • All states wanted a republic. • Many Americans feared a strong central government would lead to oppressive rule.
2. Threats to rights and freedoms • The British passed tax laws without the consent of the colonists. • The British searched homes and businesses of the colonists for smuggled goods. • The British suspended New York's assembly because New York refused to pay to house British troops.	**2. Areas of disagreement among colonists** • Whether each state should have one vote or the number of votes should based on population • Whether the national government or the state governments should control lands west of the Appalachians
	3. How these issues were resolved in the Articles of Confederation • National government was given just a few powers—to wage war, to make peace, to sign treaties, and to issue money. • National government was run by a Confederation Congress, with each state having one vote. • Most important powers were left to the states—the authority to set taxes, enforce national laws, and control lands west of the Appalachians.

Name ______________________ Date ____________

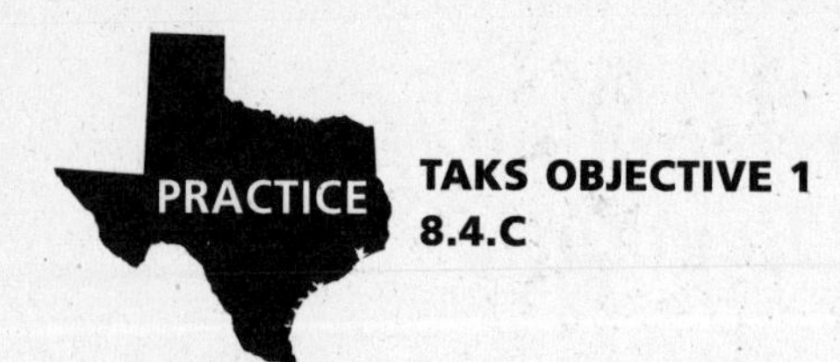

TAKS OBJECTIVE 1
8.4.C

Issues Surrounding the American Revolution

Directions: Read the following questions and choose the best answer from among the four alternatives.

1 The American colonies grew resistant to British rule because the British—

A imposed taxes without the colonists' consent

B sent troops to enforce laws and required the colonies to support the troops

C searched homes and businesses for smuggled goods

D All of the above

2 The Revolutionary War was fought mainly over the issue of—

F religious freedom

G who would control the colonies

H democracy versus communism

J freedom of the press

3 Under the Articles of Confederation, the national government had few powers because—

A Americans feared a strong national government would lead to tyranny

B the states wanted a republican government

C it was patterned after Britain's government

D George Washington insisted on it

4 Which of the following was not an area of disagreement among the colonists in framing the Articles of Confederation?

F The states should all have one vote.

G The national government should control lands west of the Appalachian Mountains.

H The government should be a republic.

J Americans needed a national government to win the war against the British.

Name ______________________ Date ____________

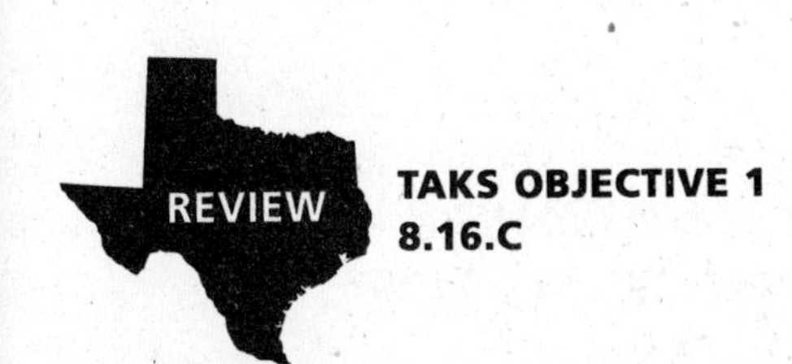

TAKS OBJECTIVE 1
8.16.C

Colonial Grievances

Learning Objective Explain the issues surrounding the American Revolution, including declaring independence and writing the Articles of Confederation. The following chart summarizes the main complaints about British rule that the colonists listed in the Declaration of Independence and tells how these complaints were addressed in the U.S. Constitution and Bill of Rights. Review this chart to answer the questions on the following page.

Colonial Grievances in Declaration of Independence	How Addressed in U.S. Constitution or Bill of Rights
Legislative Issues • Suspending colonies' legislatures and abolishing colonies' laws • Not allowing colonies' legislatures to meet regularly • Imposing taxes without colonists' consent	**Legislative** • Article 4, Section 4, guarantees every state a republican form of government. • Article 1, Section 4, specifies that Congress shall meet every year. • Article 1, Section 8, gives the authority to impose taxes to Congress.
Judicial Issues • Refusing to approve laws for establishing an independent judiciary and making judges subservient to the king • Depriving colonists of trial by jury • Transporting colonists overseas to be tried for made-up offenses	**Judicial** • Article 3 establishes an independent judiciary. • Article 3 as well as Amendment 7 proscribes trial by jury in civil cases. • Amendment 5 establishes a person's right to due process of law, and Amendment 6 establishes the right to a speedy trial in the state or district where the crime occurred.
Military Issues • Keeping standing armies without legislative consent • Quartering troops among colonists	**Military** • Article 1, Section 8, gives Congress, not the president, the authority to raise and support armies and militias and to wage war. • Amendment 3 outlaws quartering troops in homes without the owners' consent.

Name ______________________ Date ______________

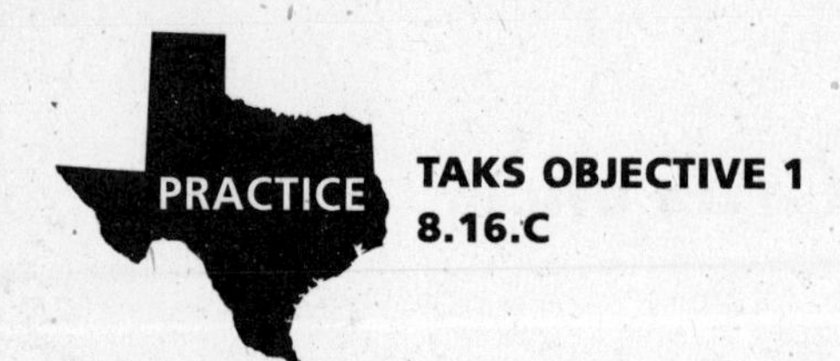

TAKS OBJECTIVE 1
8.16.C

Colonial Grievances

Directions: Read the following questions and choose the best answer from among the four alternatives.

1 Which of the following was a colonial grievance listed in the Declaration of Independence?

A Not allowing religious freedom in the colonies

B Selling titles of nobility

C Quartering troops in colonists' homes

D Pardoning convicted criminals

2 The framers of the U.S. Constitution addressed another colonial grievance by—

F giving Congress the authority to impose taxes

G giving the president the authority to impose taxes

H outlawing taxes altogether

J requiring all the people to vote directly on any new taxes

3 Amendment 7 addressed a colonial grievance by establishing the—

A right to trial by a judge in civil cases

B right to trial by jury in civil cases

C right to any kind of trial a defendant wants

D right to appeal the decision of a judge

4 How did the U.S. Constitution address the colonial grievance that legislatures were not allowed to meet regularly?

F Article 1, Section 4, specifies that Congress shall meet every year.

G Article 1, Section 4, specifies that Congress shall meet every two years.

H Article 3 establishes an independent judiciary.

J Article 6 specifies that the president should decide when Congress meets.

Name ______________________ Date ____________

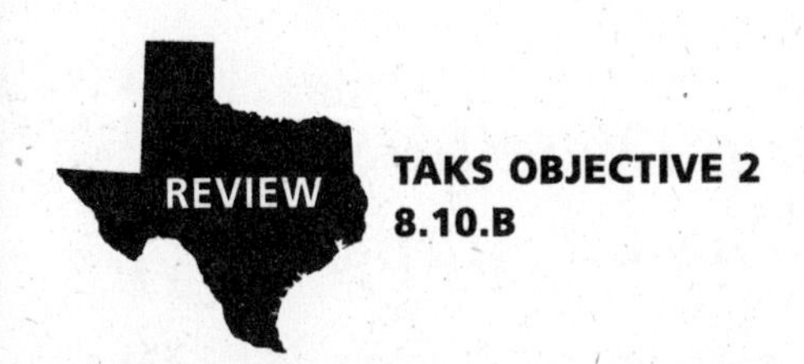

TAKS OBJECTIVE 2
8.10.B

Geographic Distributions and Patterns on Maps

Learning Objective Answer questions about geographic distributions and patterns shown on maps, graphs, and charts. The following maps are typical of the kinds you may encounter on a test. Read and apply the tips below to help you identify geographic distributions and patterns on such maps.

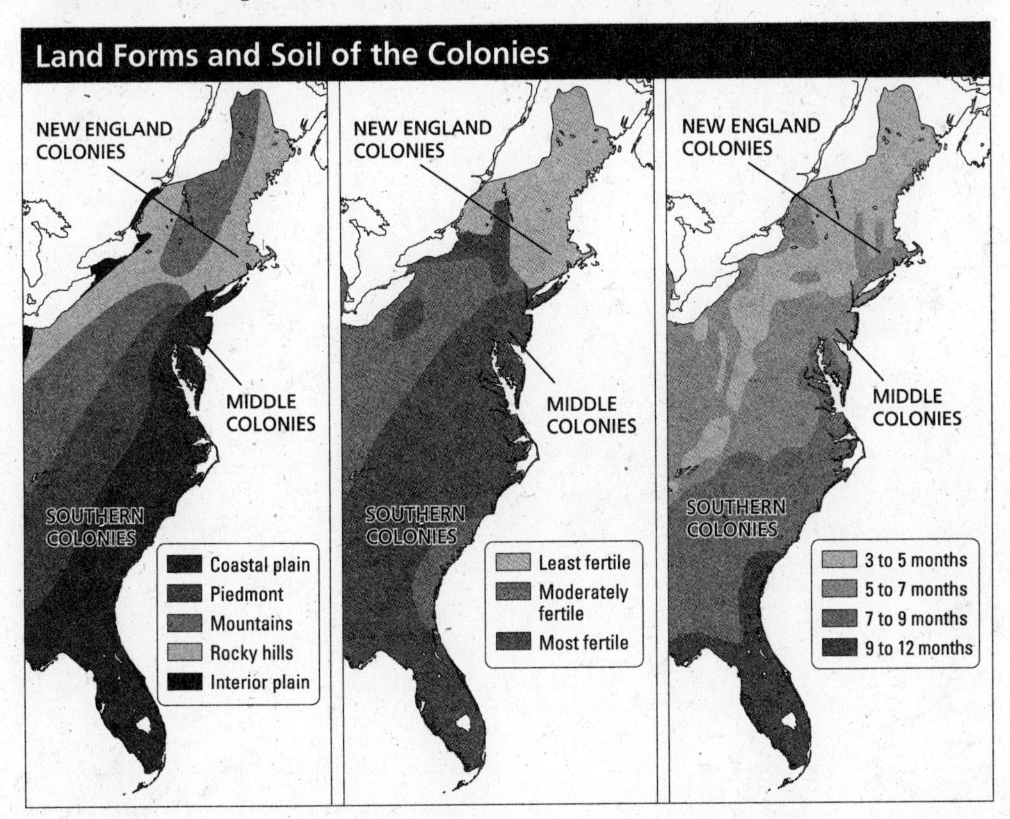

How to Answer Questions about Geographic Distributions and Patterns on Maps

1. Read the title to identify the subject and purpose of the map. The two maps above show the land forms and soil types in the three groups of American colonies.
2. Study the legend to find the meaning of the symbols used on the map. For example, on the first map key, dots indicate coastal plain.
3. Look at the symbols on the map and identify the distribution, which is simply where something is. For example, on the land forms map, you can see that the coastal plain extends along the coast of both the Southern and the Middle colonies.
4. Next, look for patterns in the distributions. For example, a pattern you can see on these maps is that the Middle and Southern colonies had the most fertile soil and the flattest land, which would make agriculture profitable there.
5. Read the test question and look back at the map to determine the answer. You may need to draw conclusions to answer the question. For example, suppose you were asked to use these maps to tell why New Englanders turned to fishing to make a living. You could conclude that, because the land was rocky and mountainous and the soil not very fertile in New England, farming was not profitable there and so the people turned to the sea to make a living.

Name ______________________ Date ______________

TAKS OBJECTIVE 2
8.10.B

Geographic Distributions and Patterns on Maps

Directions: Use the map below to answer the questions.

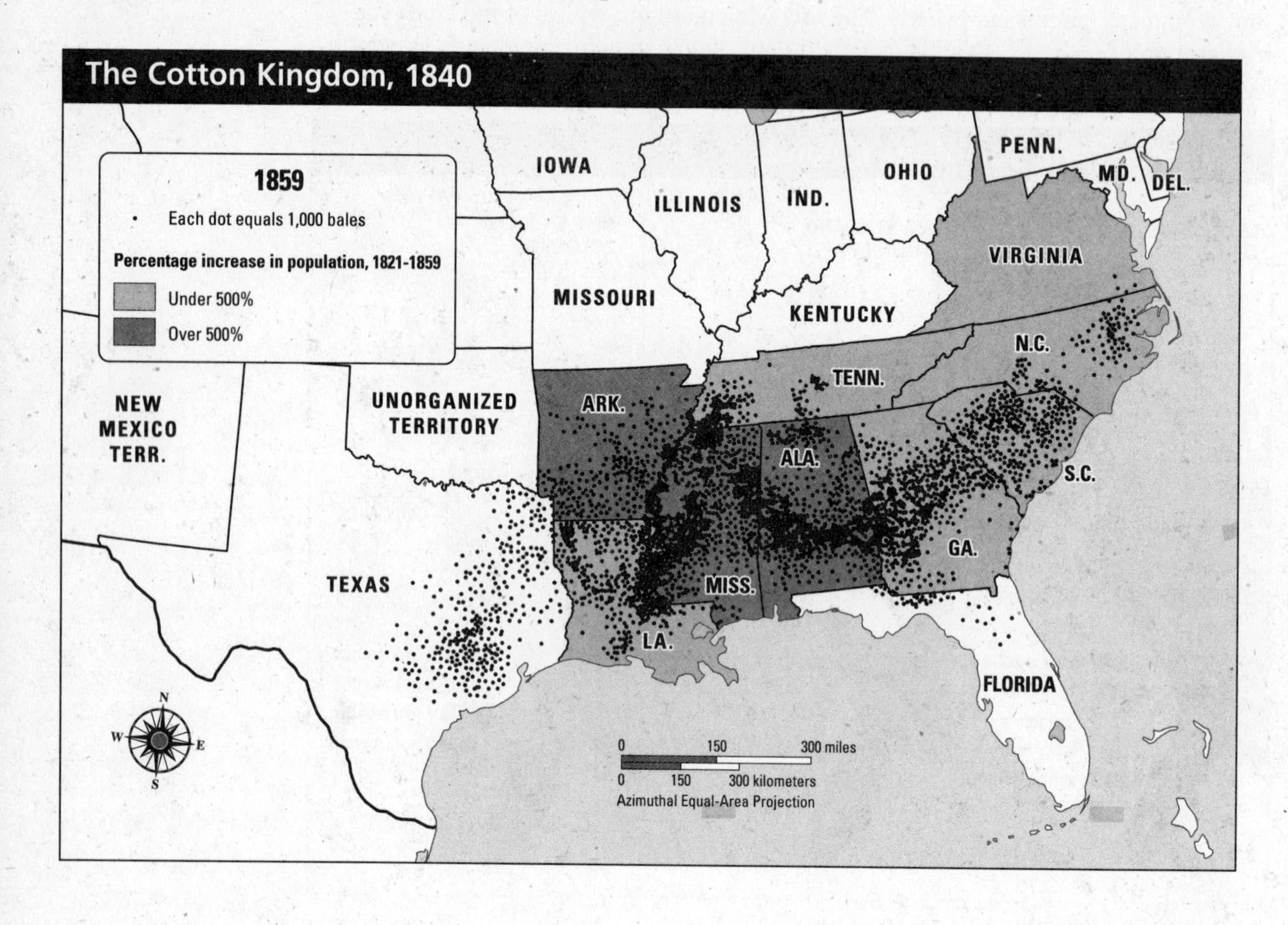

1 In what region of the country was the Cotton Kingdom of the 1800s located?

A Northeast

B Midwest

C Southeast

D Southwest

2 Growing and harvesting cotton was highly labor intensive, and large plantation owners relied on slave labor to do the work. Which of the following states probably had the largest concentration of enslaved African Americans?

F Florida

G Arkansas

H Louisiana

J Kentucky

Name ________________________________ Date ______________

TAKS OBJECTIVE 2
8.10.B

Geographic Distributions and Patterns on Graphs

Learning Objective Answer questions about geographic distributions and patterns shown on maps, graphs, and charts. The following pie graph and bar graph are typical of the kinds you may encounter on a test. Read and apply the tips below to help you identify geographic distributions and patterns on such graphs.

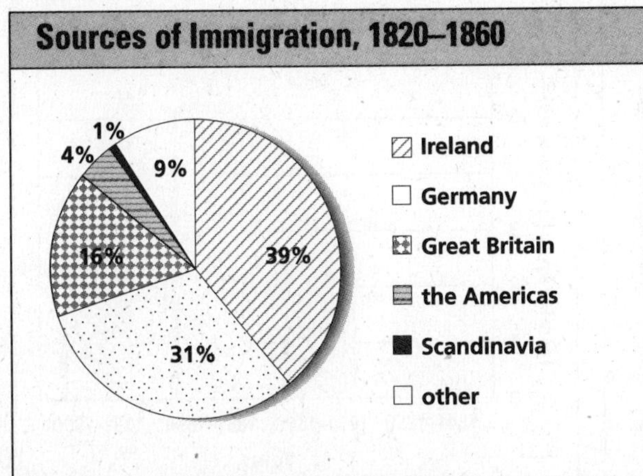

SOURCE: *Historical Statistics of the United States*

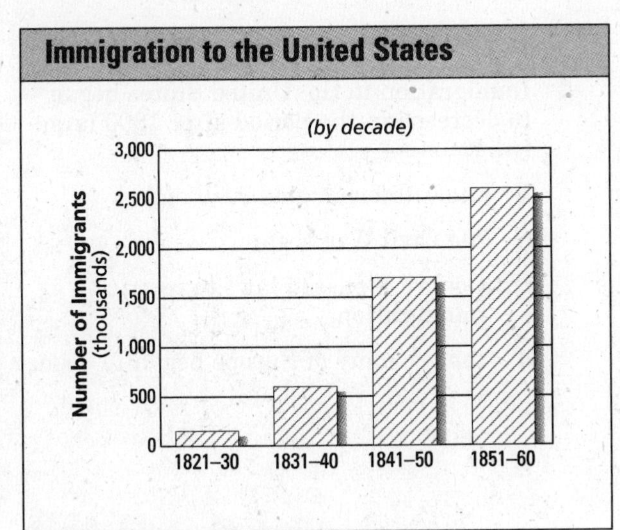

SOURCE: *Historical Statistics of the United States*

How to Answer Questions about Geographic Distributions and Patterns on Graphs

1. Read the title and the labels to identify the subject of the graph. This pie graph shows the country of origin for immigrants to the United States between 1820 and 1860. The bar graph shows how many immigrants came in each decade of the period.
2. Study the distributions shown on each graph. For example, on the pie graph, the distributions would be the actual percentages of each group of immigrants. On the bar graph, the distributions would be the actual number of immigrants in each decade.
3. Next, look for patterns in the distributions. For example, you can see from the pie graph that the largest group of immigrants came from Ireland. The bar graph shows that the number of immigrants increased during each decade of the period.
4. Read the test question and look back at the graph to determine the answer. You may need to combine information you already know with what is shown on the graph or draw conclusions to answer the question. For example, suppose you were asked to identify the largest group of immigrants to the United States between 1820 and 1860 and tell why they came to the United States. From the graph, you can see that the Irish made up the largest group. From studying history, you might remember that many Irish emigrated from their homeland to avoid starvation during the Irish Potato Famine, which occurred during this period.

Name ______________________ Date ____________

TAKS OBJECTIVE 2
8.10.B

Geographic Distributions and Patterns on Graphs

Directions: Use the graphs below and your knowledge of social studies to answer the following questions.

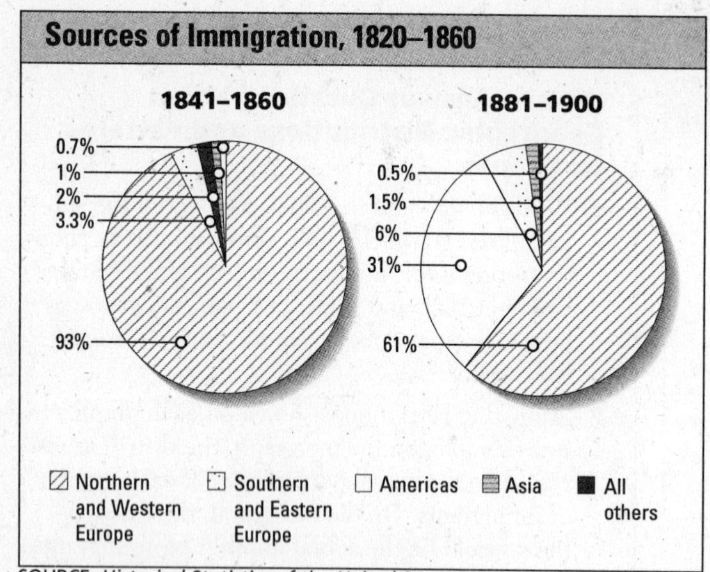

SOURCE: *Historical Statistics of the United States*

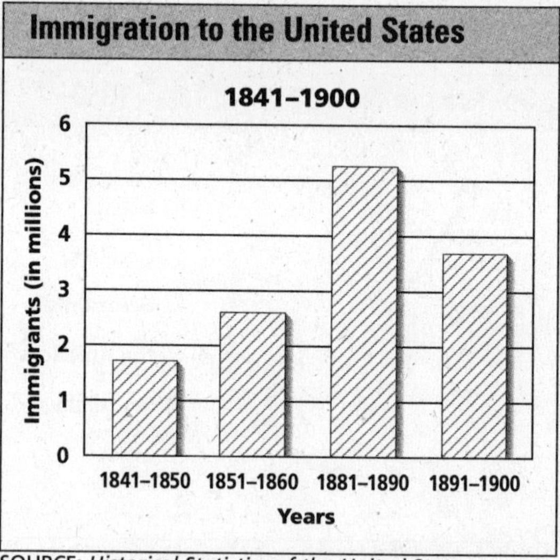

SOURCE: *Historical Statistics of the United States*

1 Which group of immigrants increased the most between 1841 and 1860 and which increased the most between 1881 and 1900?

A Northern and Western Europeans

B Southern and Eastern Europeans

C Latin Americans

D Asians

2 Immigration to the United States began to decrease in the period after 1890 largely because—

F the California gold rush ended

G the Civil War began

H Congress passed laws to restrict immigration

J the economy of Europe began to boom

Name ______________________ Date ____________

TAKS OBJECTIVE 2
8.10.B

Geographic Distributions and Patterns on Charts

Learning Objective Answer questions about geographic distributions and patterns shown on maps, graphs, and charts. The following chart is typical of the kinds you may encounter on a test. Read and apply the tips below to help you identify geographic distributions and patterns on such charts.

Import of Slaves by the Colonies, 1772			
	from Africa	from West Indies	from Continental Colonies
New Hampshire	0	4	0
Massachusetts	0	0	4
Rhode Island	0	2	0
New York	19	4	0
Maryland	86	82	7
Virginia	1,271	794	39
North Carolina	0	145	10
South Carolina	5,145	2,027	29
Georgia	117	69	142
Total	6,638	3,127	231

How to Answer Questions about Geographic Distributions and Patterns on Charts

1. Read the title and the headings to identify the subject of the chart. This chart shows the number of slaves imported by the colonies from Africa, the West Indies, and other colonies in 1772.
2. Study the distributions shown on the chart—the actual number of slaves imported by each colony from the three areas.
3. Next, look for patterns in the distributions. For example, one pattern you can see from the chart is that the southern colonies imported many more slaves than the northern and middle colonies.
3. Read the test question and look back at the chart to determine the answer. You may need to combine information you already know with what is shown on the chart. Then compare information or draw conclusions to answer the question. For example, suppose you were asked to draw a conclusion about the importation of slaves in the different colonial regions. By comparing the numbers, you might conclude that all the regions imported slaves, but the southern colonies imported far more than the northern and middle colonies.

Name ______________________ Date ______________

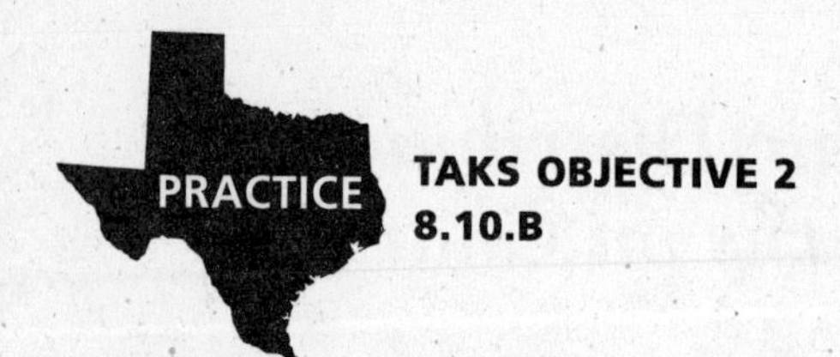

TAKS OBJECTIVE 2
8.10.B

Geographic Distributions and Patterns on Charts

Directions: Use the chart below and your knowledge of social studies to answer the following questions.

Slaves Imported to the Americas, 1601–1810 (in thousands)

Region/Country	1601–1700	1701–1810
British N. America	*	348.0
British Caribbean	263.7	1,401.3
French Caribbean	155.8	1,348.4
Spanish America	292.5	578.6
Dutch Caribbean	40.0	460.0
Danish Caribbean	4.0	24.0
Brazil (Portugal)	560.0	1,891.4

*=less than 1,000

SOURCE: Philip D. Curtin, *The Atlantic Slave Trade*

1 To which of the following regions were the most slaves imported during the period shown?

A North America

B The Caribbean

C Spanish America

D Brazil

2 Why were so many slaves imported to this region?

F They were needed to work on cotton plantations.

G They were needed to work on sugar plantations.

H They were needed as domestic workers in the homes of the wealthy.

J They were needed to work in factories.

Name ______________________ Date ______________

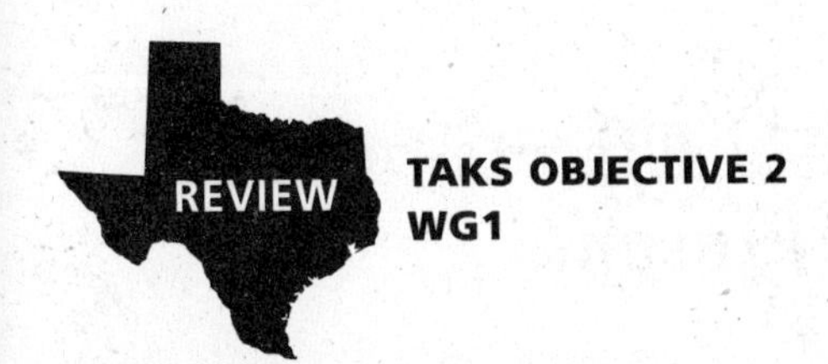

TAKS OBJECTIVE 2
WG1

Geographic Effects on the Past and Present

Learning Objective Analyze the effects of physical and human geographic patterns and processes on events in the past and describe their effects on present conditions, including significant physical features and environmental conditions that influenced migration patterns in the past and shaped the distribution of culture groups today.

One of the major migrations in world history was that of European explorers and settlers to the Americas. The map and text below summarize the physical features and environmental conditions that influenced this migration and helped to shape the distribution of culture groups today. Review this information and then answer the questions on the next page.

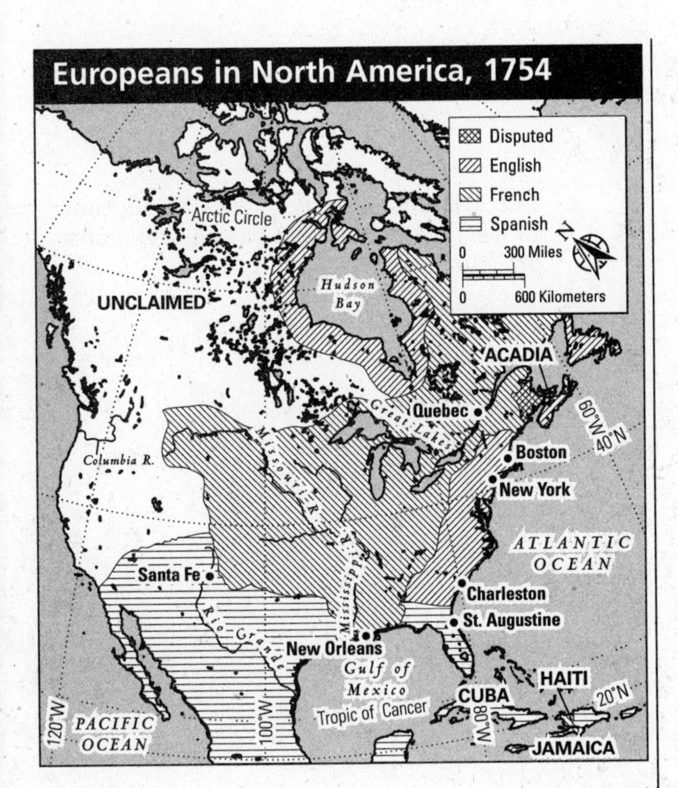

European Migration to the Americas

Initially, the drive for wealth brought European explorers to the Americas in the late 1400s. They were searching for a direct sea route to the riches of Asia. Although Europeans did not find the trade route they were searching for, they did find vast new lands. The immense natural resources of the New World—its furs, fish, gold, silver, timber, and land—attracted colonists from many nations of Europe. This map shows the lands claimed in the mid-1700s by the three main groups of European colonists—the Spanish, French, and English.

The effects of early European migration to the Americas can still be seen in the distribution of culture groups today. You will notice on the map above that the Spanish claimed most of what is today the southwestern United States, Florida, Central America, and northern South America. Today, many people of partly Spanish descent live in these areas. French culture still thrives in Quebec, Canada, and in Louisiana, where many descendants of French colonists called Cajuns live. The eastern seaboard of the United States, as well as the rest of the country, has many descendants of English and other European immigrants.

Name ______________________________ Date ______________

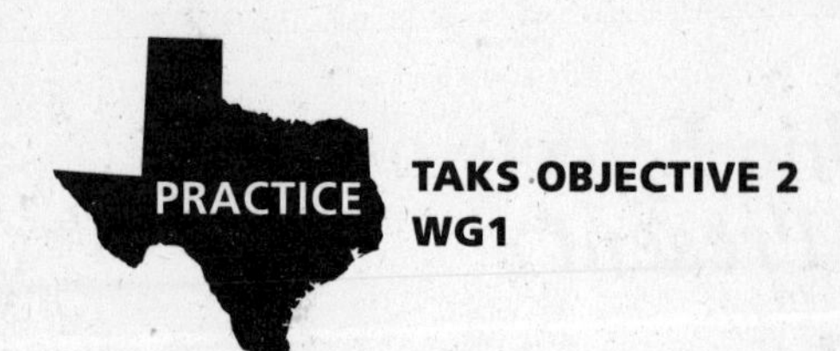

TAKS OBJECTIVE 2
WG1

Geographic Effects on the Past and Present

Directions: Read the following questions and choose the best answer from among the four alternatives.

1 The first European explorers of the New World were looking for—

A land for farming

B places to establish colonies

C a direct sea route to Asia

D a direct sea route to Africa

2 What physical features of the New World attracted explorers and settlers from Europe?

F Its plentiful supply of fur-bearing animals

G Its vast forests and land for farming

H Its gold and silver

J All of the above

3 The effects of Spanish colonization can still be seen especially in which part of the United States?

A Southwest

B Northwest

C Midwest

D Northeast

4 Descendants of early French immigrants to North America who live in Louisiana are known as—

F Mestizos

G Cajuns

H Puritans

J Loyalists

Name ____________________ Date ____________

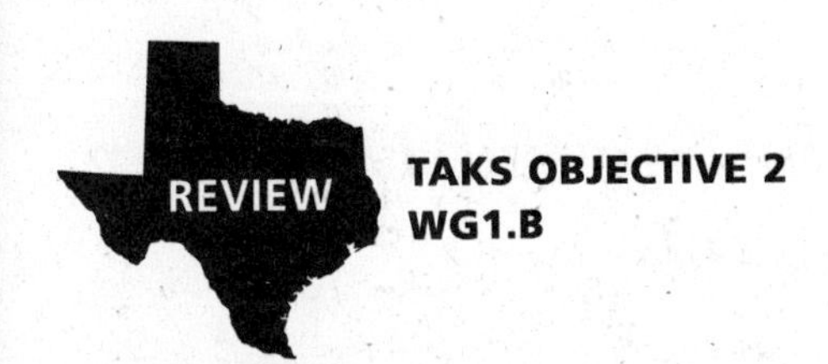

TAKS OBJECTIVE 2
WG1.B

Tracing the Spatial Diffusion of Phenomena

Learning Objective Trace the spatial diffusion of a phenomenon and describe its effects on regions of contact, such as the spread of bubonic plague and the diffusion and exchange of foods between the New and Old Worlds.

The map and text below describe how the bubonic plague spread from Asia through Europe and the effects it had on the population of Europe. Review the map and text to answer the questions on the next page.

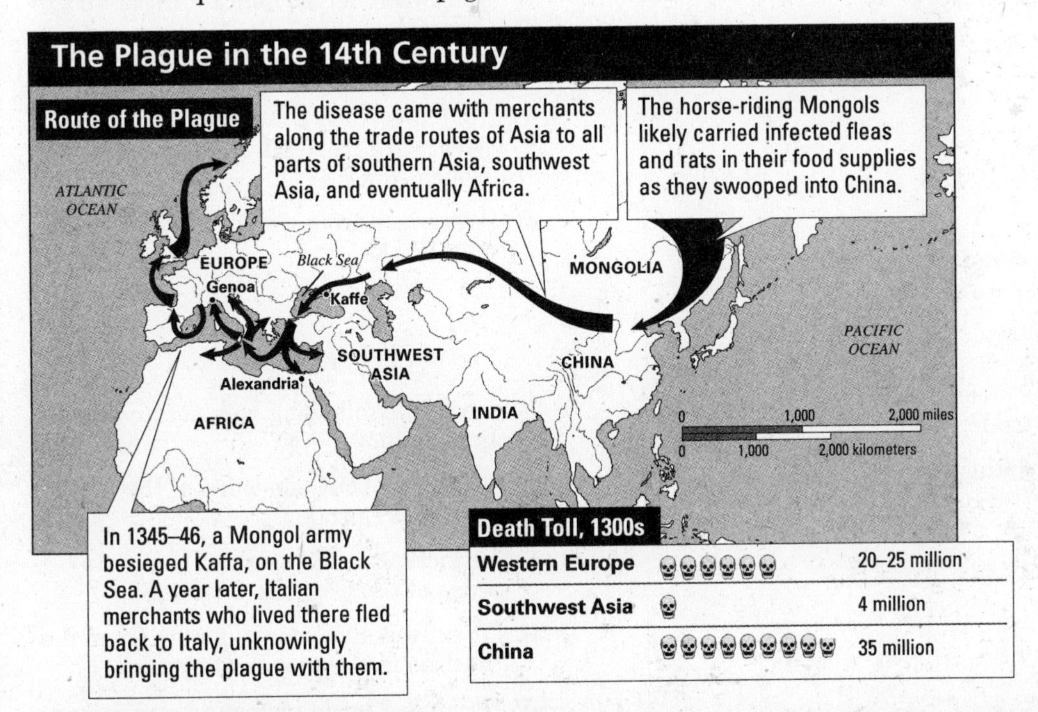

Spread of the Plague	Effects of the Plague
• Horse-riding Mongols probably carried infected fleas and rats in their food supplies when they invaded China.	• It wiped out about one-third of Europe's population.
• Merchants carried the disease along Asian trade routes to all parts of southern Asia, southwest Asia, and eventually Africa.	• As the population fell, trade declined and prices rose.
• In 1345–1346, a Mongol army invaded the city of Kaffa on the Black Sea. A year later, Italian merchants from Kaffa brought the plague back to Italy.	• The lack of workers broke down the manorial system.
• From Italy, the disease followed trade routes to France, Germany, England, and other parts of Europe.	• People became disillusioned with the Catholic Church, pessimistic about the future, and preoccupied with pleasure.

Name ______________________ Date ____________

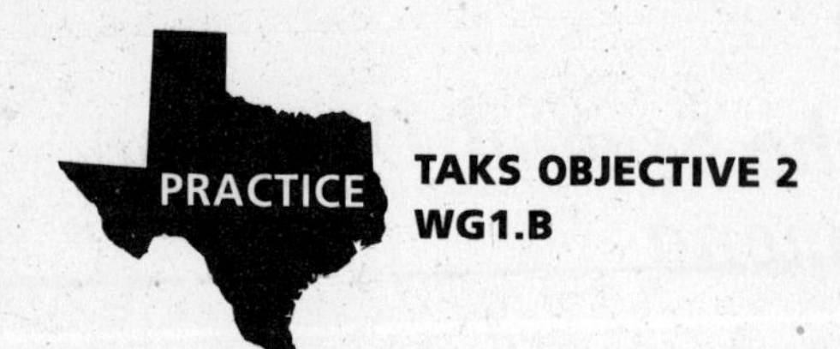

TAKS OBJECTIVE 2
WG1.B

Tracing the Spatial Diffusion of Phenomena

Directions: Read the following questions and choose the best answer from among the four alternatives.

1 Where did the bubonic plague originate?

A Kaffa on the Black Sea

B Mongolia

C Africa

D Europe

2 The bubonic plague spread across Asia and Europe as a result of—

F exploration

G migration

H war and trade

J climatic change

3 Which of the following describes the route that the plague took?

A Eastward across Asia to Africa and Europe

B Westward from Africa to Europe and Asia

C Westward from Europe to North and South America

D Westward from the New World to the Old World

4 Which of the following was not an effect of the plague?

F It killed about one-third of the population of Europe.

G It increased the prestige and influence of the Catholic Church.

H It caused a shortage of workers and a decline in the manorial system.

J It caused trade to decline and prices to rise.

Name ______________________________ Date ______________

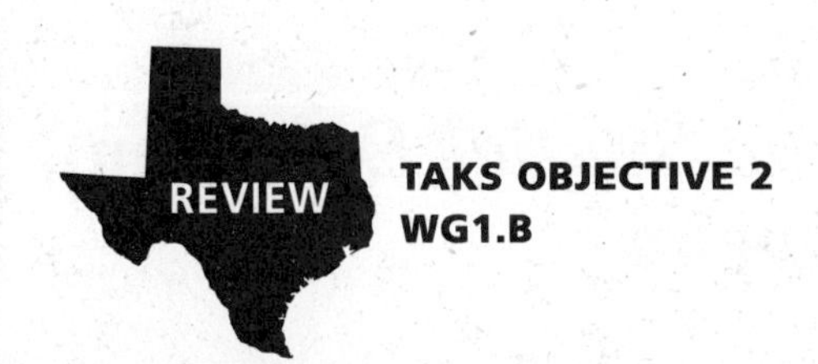

TAKS OBJECTIVE 2
WG1.B

Tracing the Spatial Diffusion of Phenomena

Learning Objective Trace the spatial diffusion of a phenomenon and describe its effects on regions of contact, such as the spread of bubonic plague or the diffusion and exchange of foods between the New and Old Worlds.

The global transfer of foods, plants, and animals during the colonization of the Americas was known as the Columbian Exchange. The infographic below shows important items in the exchange, and the chart describes some of the effects. Review the graphic and the chart to answer the questions on the next page.

The Columbian Exchange

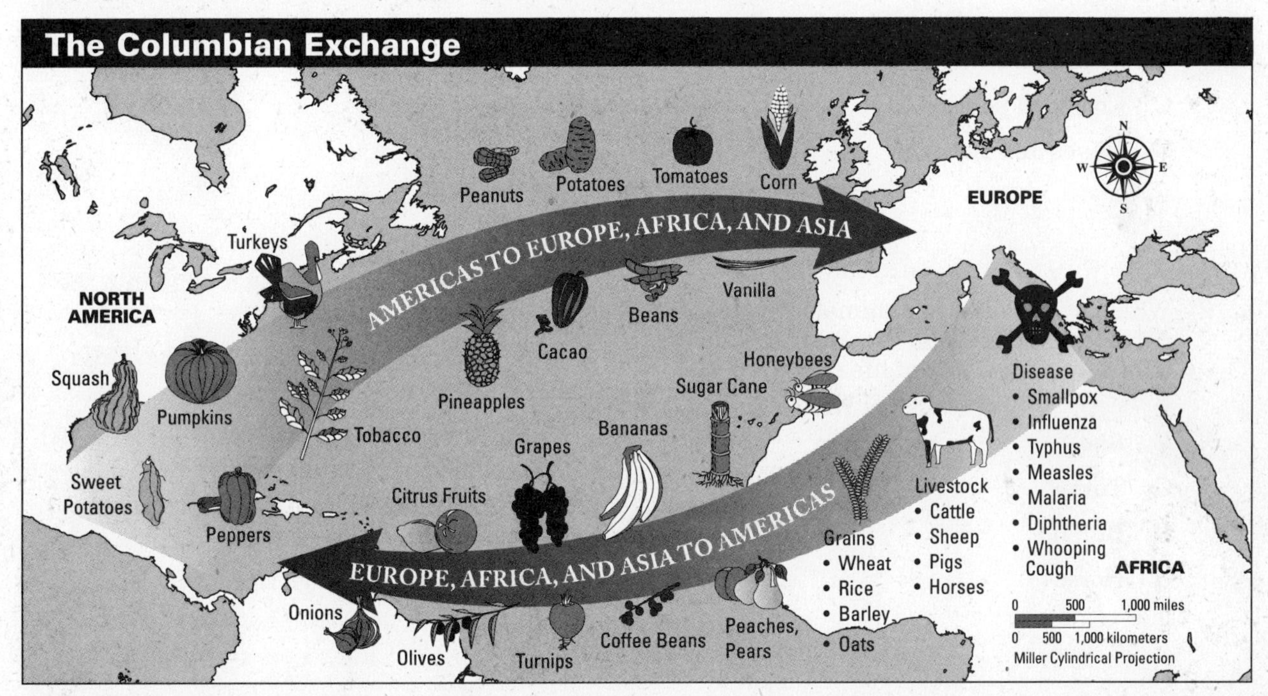

Some Effects of the Columbian Exchange on the Americas	Some Effects of the Columbian Exchange on Europe, Africa, and Asia
• The horse transformed the way of life of the Native Americans living on the Great Plains, making them nomadic hunters. • Sugar plantations in the Caribbean region made Europeans rich but led to the enslavement of many Africans. The importation of African slaves to work on the sugar plantations changed the ethnic makeup of much of Latin America. • New grains, vegetables, and fruits enhanced the native diet. • Grazing mammals destroyed natural vegetation.	• Corn and potatoes, inexpensive to grow and highly nutritious, helped people to live healthier and longer lives, boosting the world's population. • Tobacco, on the other hand, harmed people's health.

Name ______________________ Date ______________

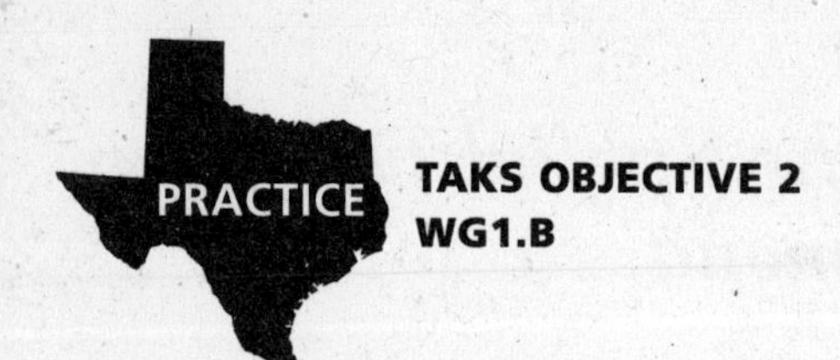

TAKS OBJECTIVE 2
WG1.B

Tracing the Spatial Diffusion of Phenomena

Directions: Read the following questions and choose the best answer from among the four alternatives.

1 Which of the following foods originated in the Americas and spread to Europe, Africa, and Asia as part of the Columbian Exchange?

A Turnips and peaches

B Sugar cane and grapes

C Corn and potatoes

D Olives and bananas

2 Which of the following animals was transported from Europe to the Americas and transformed the way of life of Native Americans on the Great Plains?

F Rat

G Turkey

H Buffalo

J Horse

3 A highly nutritious food that helped boost the population of Europe after it was introduced from the Americas was—

A the potato

B the banana

C the peach

D wheat

4 The introduction of sugar cane into the Caribbean region led to—

F an increase in the incidence of diabetes

G the importation of African slaves to work on large plantations

H an increase in Asian immigrants to the Americas

J a labor shortage in Europe

Name ______________________________ Date ______________

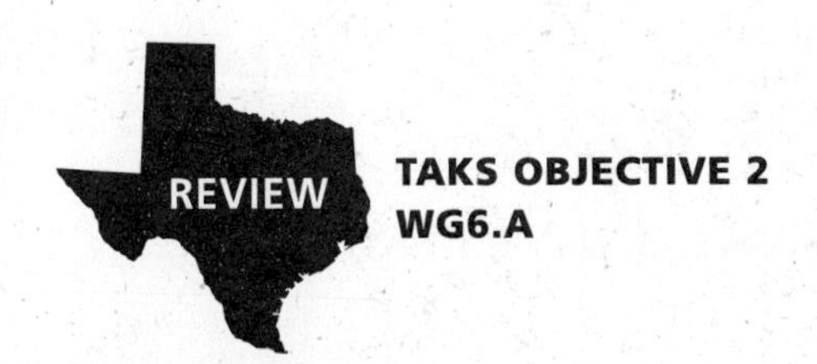

TAKS OBJECTIVE 2
WG6.A

Identifying Size and Distribution Patterns

Learning Objective Observe patterns in the size and distribution of cities using maps, graphics, and other information.

This map shows the location and size of the world's ten largest cities. Below the map are tips to help you identify patterns in the size and distribution of cities. Review the map and tips and apply what you learn to answer the questions on the next page.

World's Ten Largest Cities

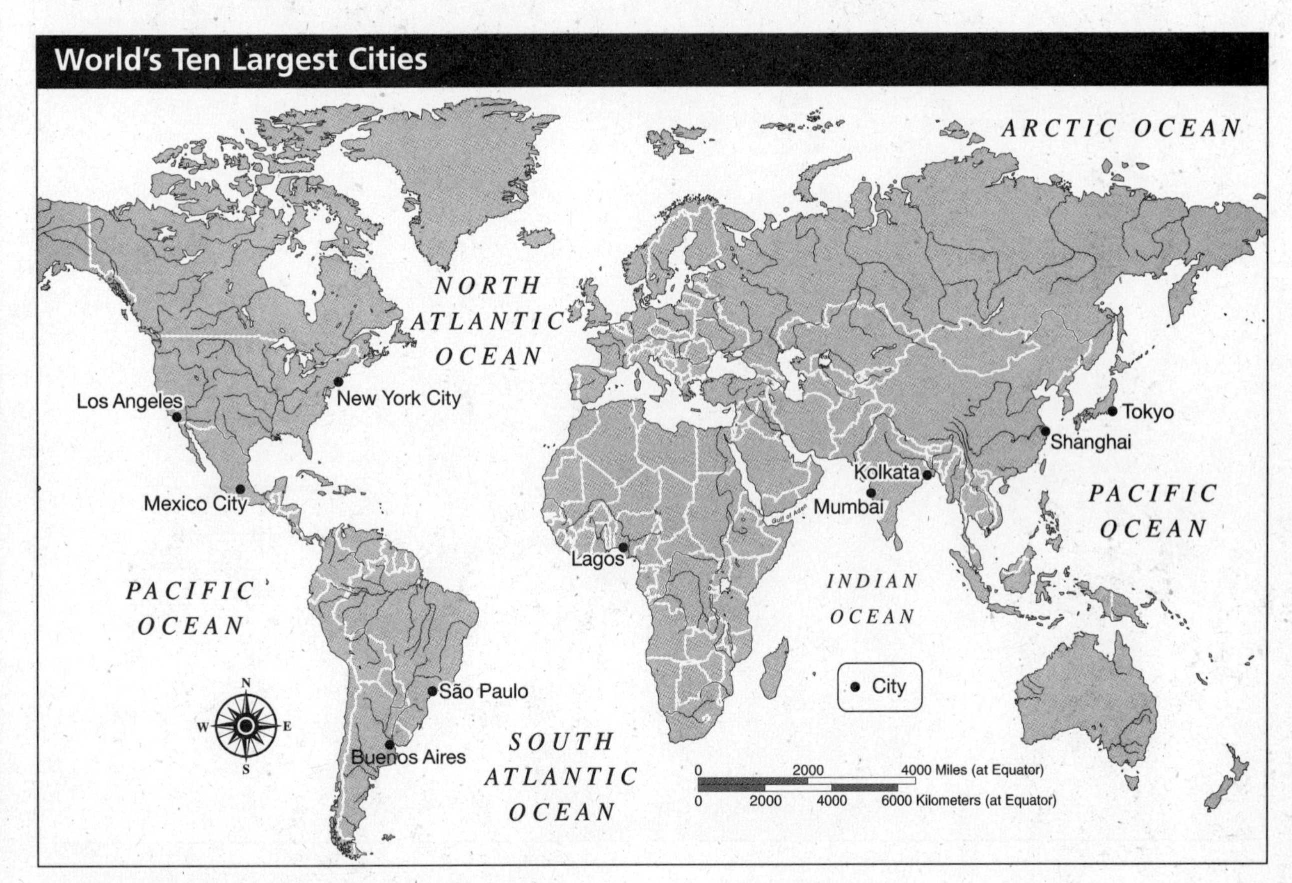

How to observe patterns in the size and distribution of cities

- Look at where the cities are located. Many cities are found in places that have a reliable water supply or have easy access to transportation, such as a river, lake, or coast. Others are found in places with access to natural resources or to such sources of energy as coal or oil. Still others have a central location that makes them a transportation hub or a good site for a capital. On this map, for example, you can see that the majority of the world's ten largest cities are located along a coast, which makes them ideally suited for trade and commerce.
- Look at the clustering of cities in certain regions. Think about why the cities are grouped in a particular area. Is the area an historic trading hub? Is the population of the region growing rapidly? On this map, you will notice that the largest percentage of cities are located in Asia, a continent with a rapidly growing population.
- Notice also where cities are not. Is the region too mountainous, too dry, or too cold to support a large population?

Name ______________________ Date ______________

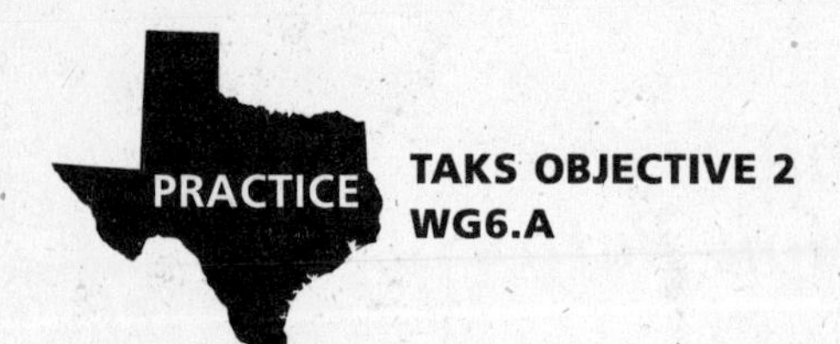

TAKS OBJECTIVE 2
WG6.A

Identifying Size and Distribution Patterns

Directions: Use the map and your knowledge of social studies to answer the following questions.

North American Cities with over Two Million People

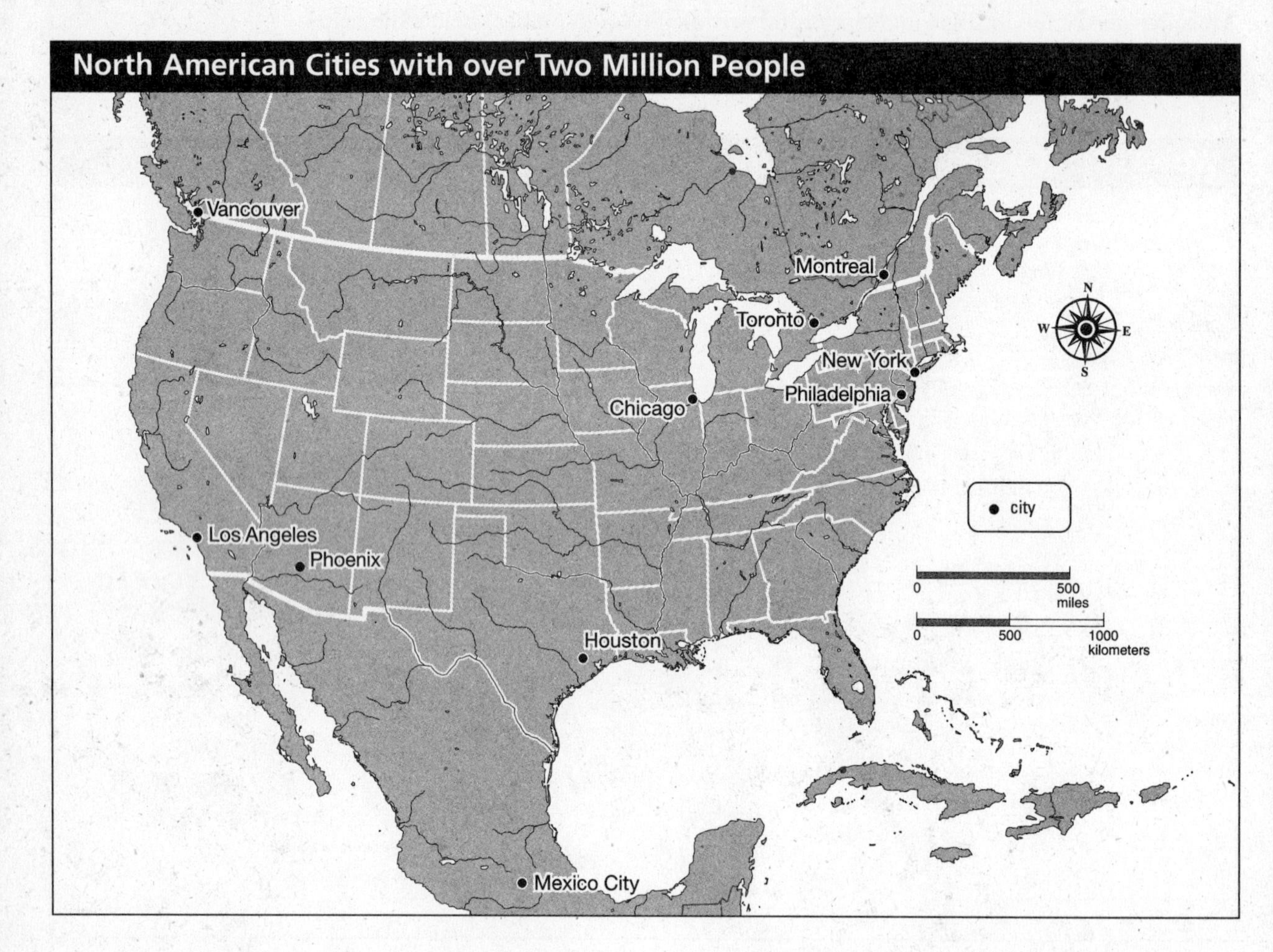

1 The majority of cities shown on this map are located—

A in Canada

B along a body of water

C on the Pacific coast

D in tropical latitudes

2 In which area of the United States are no large cities located and why?

F The Southeast because the climate is too hot

G The Northwest because the climate is too wet

H The central West because much of the land is mountainous and the climate dry

J The Midwest because the region is so far from any coast

Name ______________________________ Date ______________

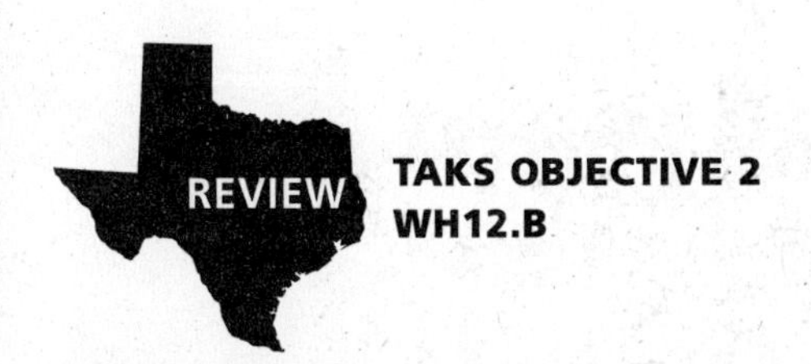

Geographic Effects on Major Historical Events

Learning Objective Analyze the effects of physical and human geographic factors on major events in world history.

The following chart gives some examples of major events in world history that were affected by geographic factors. Review the chart to answer the questions on the next page.

Major Events in World History	Effects of Geographic Factors
• Mongols' attempt to invade Japan in 1281	• In their attempt to invade Japan, the Mongols mounted the largest seaborne invasion in history at the time. The invasion was doomed by the powerful winds of a typhoon that destroyed Mongol ships and killed many sailors.
• England's defeat of the Spanish Armada in 1588	• A change in the wind and stormy weather helped the English defeat the Spanish Armada. After the Spanish sailing ships were blown off course by a change in the wind, stormy weather caused many ships to wreck off the rocky coasts of Scotland. The defeat of the Armada dealt a blow to Spain's dominance on the seas and allowed the rest of Europe to make inroads in the Americas.
• Napoleon's invasion of Russia in 1812	• As Napoleon advanced on Moscow, the Russians set fire to the city. Napoleon captured the city, but then the bitterly cold Russian winter set in. The French general had no choice but to retreat from the city to feed and shelter his army during the winter. The cold weather helped to kill more than 90,000 of Napoleon's soldiers.
• Battle of Stalingrad in 1942	• Once again the cold Russian winter played a role in thwarting an invasion. During World War II, the Russians trapped the German army inside the city of Stalingrad and cut off their supplies during the onset of winter. The few freezing, starving German soldiers who survived the siege finally had to surrender.
• Battles in North Africa during World War II (1939–1945)	• Control of Egypt and the Suez Canal was a key goal in the fighting between the Allied and Axis powers. The location of the Suez Canal made it a gateway to the oil fields of Southwest Asia. It also provided Great Britain with the shortest sea route to Asia. First Italy and then Germany fought the British to gain control of the area. However, Allied forces maintained control of the canal.

Name ______________________________ Date ______________

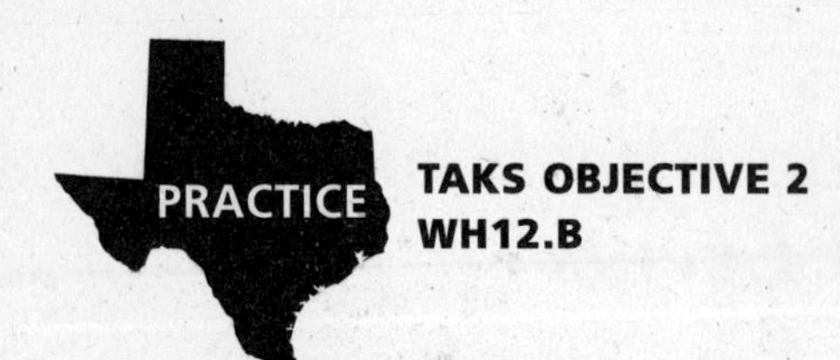

TAKS OBJECTIVE 2
WH12.B

Geographic Effects on Major Historical Events

Directions: Read the following questions and choose the best answer from among the four alternatives.

1 Both Napoleon's invasion of Russia in 1812 and the German invasion of Russia during World War II were thwarted partly by—

A the constant rainy weather

B the mountainous terrain of western Russia

C the severely cold Russian winter

D the desert heat in eastern Russia

2 Which of the following geographic factors helped the Japanese ward off an invasion by the Mongols in 1281?

F Earthquake

G Volcanic eruption

H Monsoon

J Typhoon

3 Why did both the Axis and the Allied countries want control of Egypt during World War II?

A Because the Suez Canal provided a gateway to both the oil fields of Southwest Asia and a short sea route to Asia

B Because Egypt had huge deposits of iron needed to build tanks and other weapons

C Because Egypt was the richest country in Africa

D Because Egypt was the gateway to conquering the rest of Africa

4 In defeating the Spanish Armada in 1588, the English were aided by—

F stormy weather off the coast of Scotland

G huge, moving icebergs in the North Sea

H a pod of whales in the North Atlantic

J freezing waters in the English Channel

Name ______________________________ Date ______________

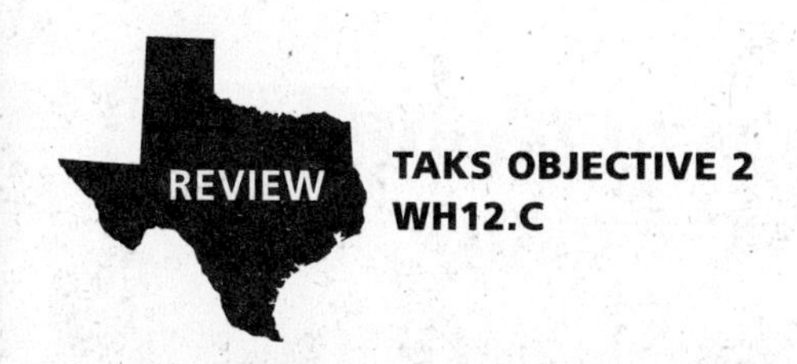

TAKS OBJECTIVE 2
WH12.C

Using Maps to Identify Geographic Factors

Learning Objective Interpret historical maps to identify and explain geographic factors that have influenced people and events in the past.

This map shows the region of the Fertile Crescent, a rich farming land where the Sumerians developed one of the world's first civilizations about 3,000 B.C. Below the map are guidelines for identifying important geographic factors on such maps. Read and apply the guidelines to help you answer questions about such maps.

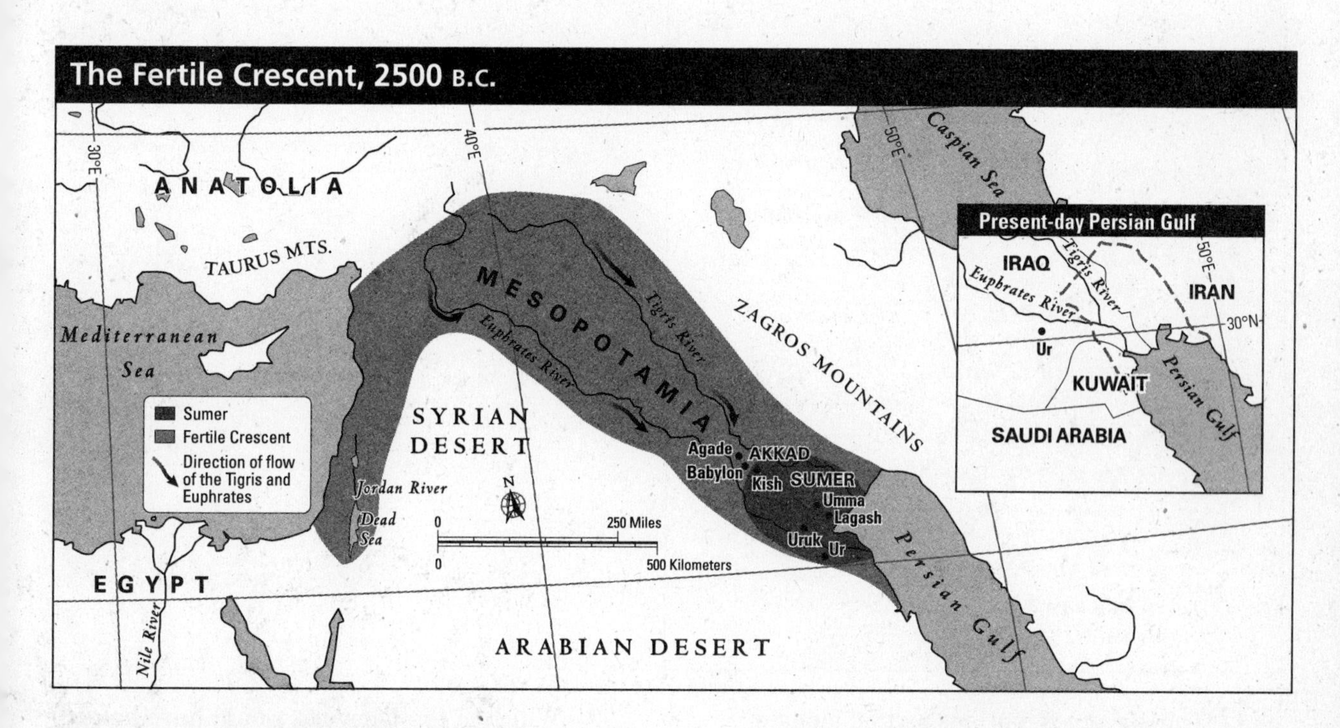

How to Interpret Historical Maps

1 Read the map's title, legend, and labels to identify what the map shows. This map shows the location and extent of the Fertile Crescent, the location of Sumer, and important physical features of the region and surrounding area.

2 Identify the main physical or political features that distinguish the region. For example, this map shows that the largest part of the Fertile Crescent consists of a plain through which the Tigris and Euphrates rivers flow. These rivers originate in mountains that border the Fertile Crescent on the north. Sumer developed near the mouth of these rivers, where they empty into the Persian Gulf.

3 Use your knowledge of social studies to explain the significance of these geographic factors. For example, you know that river valleys typically provide fertile land for farming. Therefore, you can conclude that the Tigris and Euphrates rivers were important geographic factors in the development of the Sumerian civilization because they supported farming settlements.

Name ______________________ Date ______________

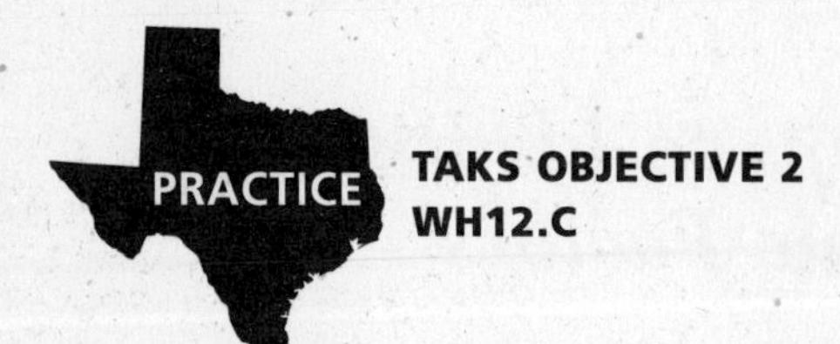

TAKS OBJECTIVE 2
WH12.C

Using Maps to Identify Geographic Factors

Directions: Use the map below and your knowledge of social studies to answer the following questions.

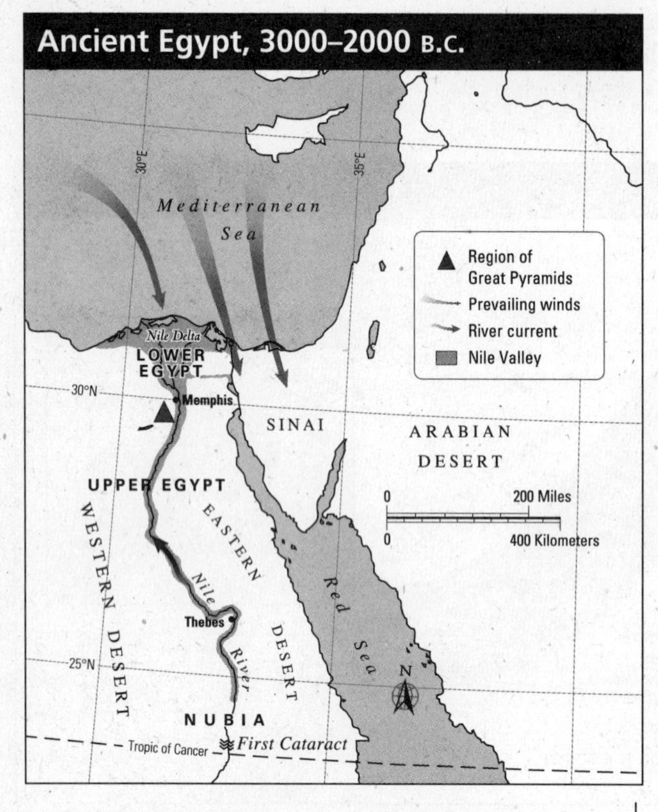

1 The ancient Egyptians settled along a narrow strip of land close to the Nile River. Which of the following statements explains why they did so?

A Only this strip of fertile land could support farming settlements in the region because the surrounding land was desert.

B The narrow valley along the Nile was surrounded by high mountains.

C Since the Nile flows south, the people wanted to live near the river to transport goods into Central Africa.

D Because the Nile's source is the Mediterranean Sea, the river does not flood and so settling along its valley posed no risk.

2 Which of the following would have helped the ancient Egyptians sail upriver from the Nile's mouth toward its source?

F Prevailing winds from the Red Sea

G The river's current

H Prevailing winds from the Mediterranean Sea

J All of the above

Name ______________________________ Date ______________

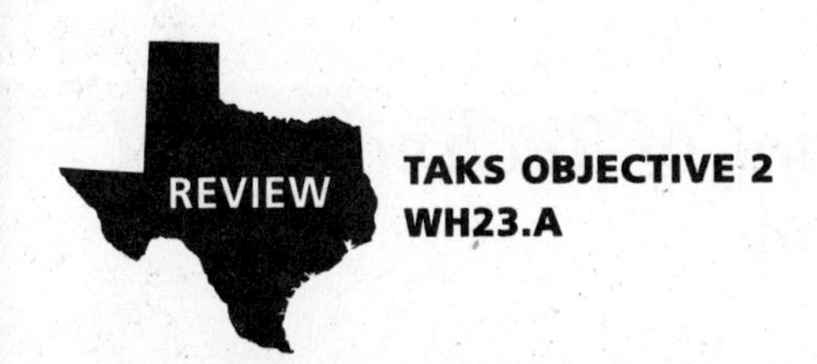

TAKS OBJECTIVE 2
WH23.A

The Impact of Technological Innovation

Learning Objective Give examples of technological innovations that occurred at different periods in history and describe the changes produced by these discoveries and innovations.

The chart below provides some examples of historic technological innovations and changes that resulted from them. Review the chart to answer the questions on the next page.

Time	Technological Innovation	Changes Produced
about 8000 B.C.	farming and farming tools	People no longer had to search for food but could settle in villages, which eventually developed into cities.
about 3500 B.C.	wheel	People could transport larger loads more easily and farther. The wheel became a basic part of many vehicles and machines.
about 3500 B.C.	writing	People could communicate over long distances and preserve information for future generations.
1100s in Europe	magnetic compass	This ancient Chinese invention reached Europe in the 1100s. It helped to make possible the long sea voyages that resulted in the discovery of the New World.
1200s in Europe	gunpowder	Gunpowder reached Europe in the 1200s and contributed to the decline of feudalism because stone castles could not be defended against cannonballs. Gunpowder changed the nature of warfare.
mid-1400s	printing	As the first means of mass communication, printing made more knowledge available to a larger number of people.
1760s	improved steam engine	The steam engine fueled the Industrial Revolution.
1830s	electricity	Electricity made possible the development of modern industry and communication and transportation systems.
1860	internal-combustion engine	This invention made possible the development of the automobile. With the automobile, people could live a long distance from where they worked, which allowed suburbs to develop.
1903	airplane	The airplane allowed people to travel frequently and over long distances for business and pleasure.
1920s	television	Television partially replaced other news sources and forms of entertainment. It influenced how people spent their time and money and took people away from other activities.
mid-1900s	computer	The computer simplified time-consuming tasks and provided organizations and individuals with a way to store and manage large amounts of information. It changed how people in almost every field did their jobs and allowed people to share information with others around the world through the Internet and e-mail.

Name ______________________ Date ______________

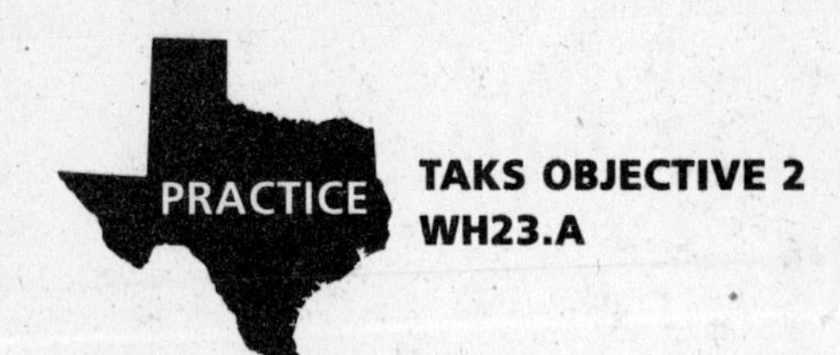

TAKS OBJECTIVE 2
WH23.A

The Impact of Technological Innovation

Directions: Read the following questions and choose the best answer from among the four alternatives.

1 Which of the following inventions reached Europe from Asia in the 1200s and contributed to the decline of feudalism?

A Wheel

B Magnetic compass

C Printing

D Gunpowder

2 Which of the following technological innovations helped make possible the long sea voyages that led to the European exploration of the New World?

F Magnetic compass

G Triangular sail

H Sternpost rudder

J All of the above

3 The development of agriculture about 8000 B.C. made it possible for nomadic hunting and gathering societies to—

A become vegetarians

B settle in villages

C own private property

D give-up hunting

4 The invention that fueled the Industrial Revolution was—

F the steam engine

G the internal combustion engine

H the computer

J the wheel

Name ______________________ Date ______________

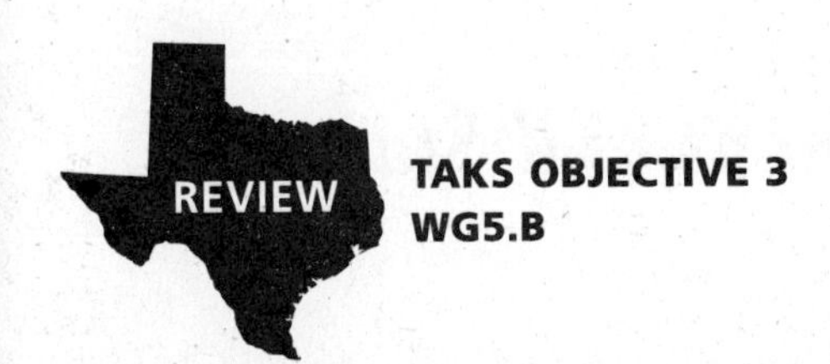

Development and Standard of Living

Learning Objective Analyze political, economic, and demographic data to determine the level of development and standard of living in a given nation.

The chart and tips below will help you analyze information about a nation's government, economy, and population to draw conclusions about its level of development and standard of living. Review the chart and tips to answer the questions on the next page.

Political, Economic, and Demographic Data on Selected Countries

Country	Government	Economic System	GDP Per Capita	Labor Force	Infant Mortality Rate (per 1,000 live births)	Life Expectancy	Literacy Rate
Cuba	Communist	command	$1,700	23% agricultural 24% industry 53% services	8	76	96%
Sweden	constitutional monarchy	market	$20,700	2% agricultural 24% industry 74% services	3	80	99%
United States	federal republic	market	$33,900	3% agricultural 24% industry 73% services	7	77	97%
Zambia	republic	mixed	$880	5% agriculture 6% industry 9% services	92	37	78%

SOURCE: *CIA World Factbook*, 2000

How to analyze the data

1 GDP per capita is the value of goods and services that a country produces per person. The higher the GDP per capita, the stronger the economy. Labor force by occupation divides the work force into three sectors. In more developed economies, a small percentage of people work in the agricultural sector, a larger percentage work in the industrial sector, and the largest percentage work in the services sector.

2 Infant mortality rate and life expectancy rate are two statistics that geographers look at to evaluate standard of living. In general, the lower the infant mortality rate and the higher the life expectancy rate, the healthier the people are and the higher the standard of living.

3 Literacy rate also gives a clue to the standard of living. A high literacy rate indicates that most citizens have access to public education.

Based on the data above, you could conclude that the United States and Sweden have highly developed economies and a high standard of living. They have a high GDP per capita and the largest percentage of the labor force working in the services sector. Their infant mortality rates are low, and their life expectancy rates are high. They also have high literacy rates.

You also could conclude that Cuba and Zambia are developing nations, but Cuba is more developed than Zambia. Both nations have a low GDP per capita. Cuba's economy, however, has a smaller majority of the people working in the services sector, while a huge percentage of Zambia's people work in agriculture. Cuba has a much lower infant mortality rate and much higher life expectancy and literacy rates than Zambia, which indicates that Cuba's people enjoy a higher standard of living than Zambia's.

Name ______________________ Date ______________

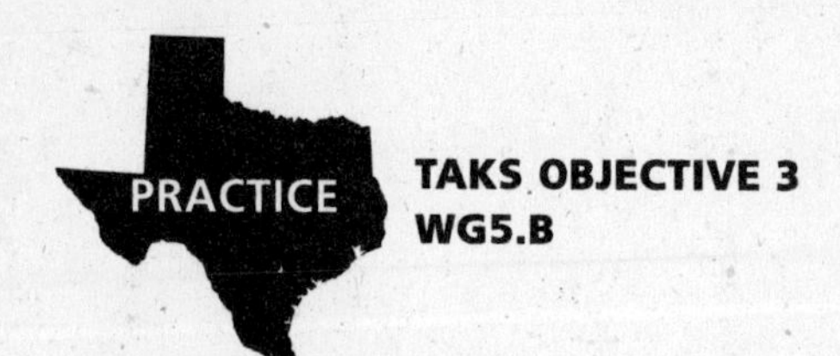

TAKS OBJECTIVE 3
WG5.B

Development and Standard of Living

Directions: Use the chart below and your knowledge of social studies to answer the following questions.

Political, Economic, and Demographic Data on Selected Countries

Country	Government	Economic System	GDP Per Capita	Labor Force	Infant Mortality Rate (per 1,000 live births)	Life Expectancy	Literacy Rate
Canada	confederation with parliamentary democracy	market	$23,300	3% agricultural 22% industry 75% services	5	79	97%
China	Communist	mixed	$3,800	50% agricultural 24% industry 26% services	29	71	82%
Great Britain	constitutional monarchy	market	$21,800	1% agricultural 19% industry 80% services	6	78	99%
Pakistan	federal republic military takeover in 1999	mixed	$2,000	44% agriculture 17% industry 39% services	82	61	38%

SOURCE: *CIA World Factbook*, 2000

1 Which of the following conclusions can you draw from this data?

A Canada has a highly developed economy and a high standard of living.

B Great Britain has a highly developed economy but a low standard of living.

C Pakistan has a higher standard of living than China.

D China has a highly developed economy but a low standard of living.

2 This data shows that Pakistan is—

F a developing country

G a developed country

H a country with a high standard of living

J a democratic country

Name ______________________ Date ______________

TAKS OBJECTIVE 3
WG10.C

Patterns of Agriculture and Industry

Learning Objective Compare the ways people satisfy their basic needs through the production of goods and services, such as subsistence agriculture versus market-oriented agriculture or cottage industries versus commercial industries.

The following charts describe the basic features of subsistence agriculture, market-oriented agriculture, cottage industries, and commercial industries. Review and compare these features to answer the questions on the next page.

Subsistence versus Market-Oriented Agriculture

Subsistence Agriculture	Market-Oriented Agriculture
• Farming is done to meet the immediate needs of the family or group. • Labor force consists of a family or small group. • Family or group is nearly self-sufficient; they meet they need.	• Farming is done to produce food to sell in a market. • Labor force varies: may be a family, small group, or hired laborers. • Farmers and buyers are interdependent; farmers earn money by selling their products and then buy what they need.
• This form of agriculture is common in Africa, Latin America, and Asia.	• This form of agriculture is common in North America and Europe.

Cottage versus Commercial Industries

Cottage Industries	Commercial Industries
• Family or small group produces goods to be sold in a market. • Work is done in the home. • Production of goods is on a small scale. • Family may meet their basic needs by producing some of what they need and buying the rest. • Cottage industries employ a few people in places throughout the world.	• Many hired laborers produce goods to be sold in a market. • Work is done in a factory or other central location. • Production of goods is on a large scale. • Workers meet their basic needs by using money they earn to buy what they need. • Commercial industries employ a large number of people and are found throughout the world.

Name ______________________ Date ____________

TAKS OBJECTIVE 3
WG10.C

Patterns of Agriculture and Industry

Directions: Read the following questions and choose the best answer from among the four alternatives.

1 In subsistence agriculture, workers produce—

A only enough food to meet their own needs

B only organically grown foods

C much more food than they need to subsist

D only foods that are dietary requirements

2 In commercial agriculture, farmers are dependent on—

F the government

G buyers

H pesticides

J price controls

3 In cottage industries, workers produce goods in—

A large groups of cottages

B factories

C private homes

D special public housing

4 A key difference between cottage and commercial industries is—

F the scale of production

G the price of goods produced

H the quality of goods produced

J the cost of labor

Name ______________________ Date ____________

TAKS OBJECTIVE 3
WG18.A

The Process of Cultural Change

Learning Objective Describe the impact of general processes such as migration, war, trade, independent inventions, and diffusion of ideas and motivations on cultural change.

The following two diagrams describe the general effects of migration and war on cultural change. Review the diagrams to answer the questions on the next page.

Impact on Cultural Change

Migration

- The population of the place of destination increases.
- The population of the place of origin decreases.
- The age and sex structure of the immigrant group changes the population structure in both the destination and origin areas. Emigrant groups often consist largely of young singles. Therefore, the place of origin loses young members of childbearing age, resulting in an aging of its population. The place of destination often has an increase in births, resulting in a reduction in the average age of the society.
- The migrating group may adopt many cultural practices of the place of destination.
- The migrating group may overwhelm or dominate the native group and impose its culture on the native area.
- The two cultures may mix to varying degrees.

War

- The population of all societies involved in the war decreases. Often there is a disproportionate decrease in the number of young males.
- The invading group may completely wipe out the conquered group or destroy much of its cultural heritage.
- The invading group may impose its culture on the conquered group.
- The invading group may adopt some cultural features of the conquered group.
- Occasionally, the invading group is assimilated into the conquered society.

Name ______________________ Date ______________

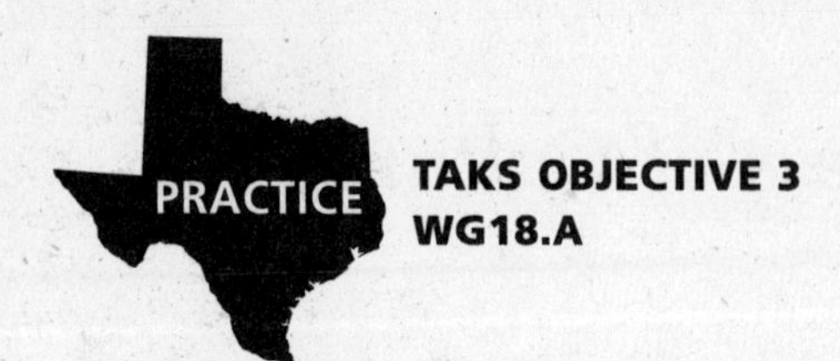

TAKS OBJECTIVE 3
WG18.A

The Process of Cultural Change

Directions: Read the following questions and choose the best answer from among the four alternatives.

1 When a large group of people migrate to another area, the population of the place of origin tends to—

A become younger

B become older

C increase

D stabilize

2 Which of the following is not a typical effect of migration?

F Mixing of cultures in the place of destination

G Domination of one culture over another in the place of destination

H Change in population structure in the place of destination

J A complete loss of culture

3 War typically results in—

A a decrease in the populations of the nations involved

B an increase in the number of young males in the warring nations

C a reduction in the average age of the populations involved

D a low mortality rate in the warring nations

4 Which of the following is not a common effect of war?

F The warring nations adopt cultural features of each other's society.

G The cultures of the warring nations are unaffected.

H The invading group imposes its culture on the conquered group.

J The invading group destroys much of the cultural heritage of the conquered group.

Name ______________________ Date ______________

TAKS OBJECTIVE 3
WG18.A

The Process of Cultural Change

Learning Objective Describe the impact of general processes such as migration, war, trade, independent inventions, and diffusion of ideas and motivations on cultural change.

The following two diagrams describe the general effects of trade, independent inventions, and diffusion of ideas and motivations on cultural change. Review the diagrams to answer the questions on the next page.

Impact on Cultural Change

Trade

- Resources, products, customs, ideas, religions, languages, art, and even diseases are exchanged.
- Societies may specialize since they can trade to obtain the things they do not produce.
- Bilingualism and multilingualism may increase to accommodate trade.
- New words may be added to native languages to accommodate the demands of trade.

Independent Inventions

- An invention may help a society respond to such pressures as growing population or the depletion of a natural resource.
- An invention may change many aspects of a society's way of life and thus have a radiating impact throughout the culture.
- A culture may develop differently from surrounding ones.
- A culture may gain a competitive edge over another.

Diffusion (spread) of Ideas and Motivations

- A group may reject the ideas of another culture, adopt them, or select among them.
- Adopting cultures may change the meaning or form of the new ideas, or create a fusion of old and new ideas.

Name ______________________ Date ______________

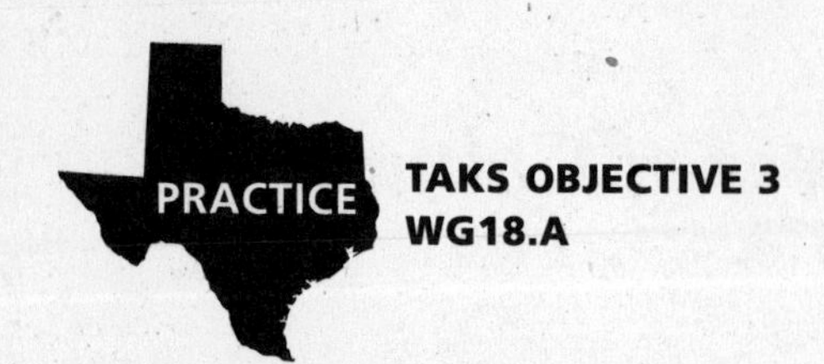

TAKS OBJECTIVE 3
WG18.A

The Process of Cultural Change

Directions: Read the following questions and choose the best answer from among the four alternatives.

1 When new ideas spread from one culture to another, the adopting culture may—

- **A** select among the ideas
- **B** change the meaning or form of the ideas
- **C** create a fusion of old and new ideas
- **D** All of the above

2 Trade may contribute to—

- **F** the diffusion of ideas and motivations
- **G** changes in language
- **H** specialization
- **J** All of the above

3 Which of the following statements best reflects the impact that independent inventions may have on a culture?

- **A** They may dramatically change a culture.
- **B** They typically have less impact than trade.
- **C** They ensure a culture's stability.
- **D** They are the most important factor in a culture's survival.

4 The automobile is an example of an invention that had—

- **F** little impact on culture
- **G** a radiating impact throughout a culture
- **H** a localized impact
- **J** a negative impact on migration

Name ______________________ Date ______________

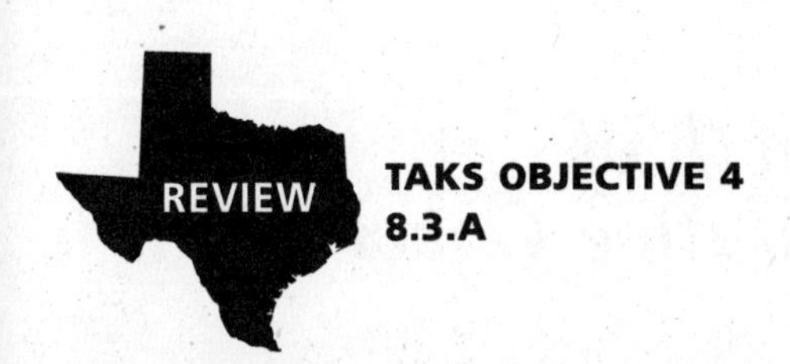

TAKS OBJECTIVE 4
8.3.A

The Growth of Representative Government

Learning Objective Explain the reasons for the growth of representative government and institutions during the colonial period.

The chart below explains why the American colonists established representative government and institutions in the New World. Review these reasons before answering the questions on the next page.

Reasons for Growth of Representative Government and Institutions in the Colonies
• English colonists expected the right to elect representatives to government because English citizens had long enjoyed this right. Because the British Parliament was far away, the colonists formed their own elected assemblies. • English colonists expected the rights granted by the Magna Carta and English Bill of Rights, such as the right to trial by a jury of peers and the right to government based on laws made by Parliament. • The colonists were influenced by the Enlightenment, which emphasized that people had natural rights and that government gets its authority from the people and should reflect their will. • The colonists wanted to make sure their rights were respected after the English king began to trample them by such acts as imposing taxes without their consent, suspending their assemblies, and housing soldiers in people's homes.

Name ______________________________ Date ______________

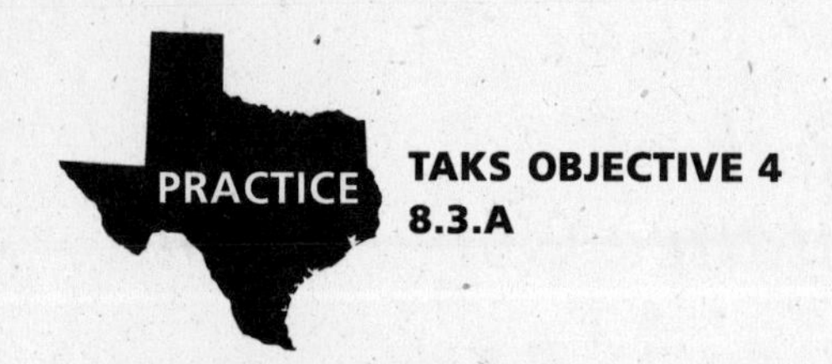

The Growth of Representative Government

Directions: Read the following questions and choose the best answer from among the four alternatives.

1 **Which of the following was a European movement that emphasized natural rights and influenced the colonists' thinking about representative government?**

A Great Awakening

B Enlightenment

C Mayflower Compact

D Glorious Revolution

2 **The colonists began to practice representative government by—**

F sending representatives to the English Parliament

G forming their own militias

H establishing their own elected assemblies

J voting directly on taxes

3 **Which of the following contributed to the English colonists' expectation of having a representative government?**

A Magna Carta

B English Bill of Rights

C English Parliament

D All of the above

4 **How did the colonists react when the English king trampled on what they considered their natural and legal rights?**

F The colonists gave up their ideas about representative government.

G The colonists' desire for their own representative government increased.

H The colonists wanted to strengthen their ties to England.

J The colonists lost faith in any form of government.

Name ________________________ Date ____________

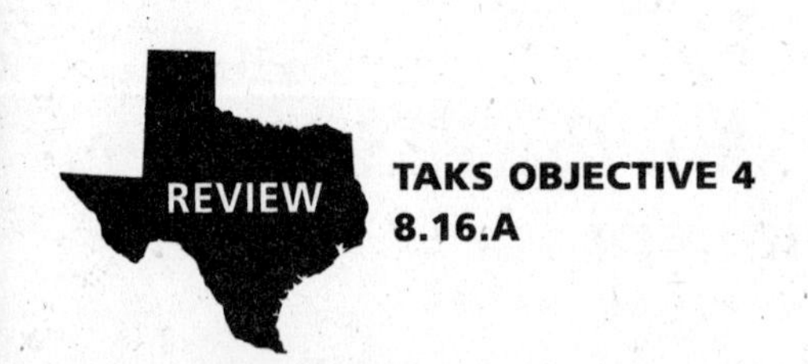

TAKS OBJECTIVE 4
8.16.A

Influences on the U.S. System of Government

Learning Objective Identify the influence of ideas from historic documents, including the Magna Carta, the English Bill of Rights, the Declaration of Independence, and the Federalist Papers, on the U.S. system of government.

The chart below describes how key ideas from the Magna Carta, the English Bill of Rights, the Declaration of Independence, and the Federalist Papers influenced the U.S. system of government. Review the chart to answer the questions on the next page.

Key Ideas in Historic Documents	Influence on U.S. System of Government
Magna Carta • right to be secure in your property • right to due process of law • right to trial by jury • no taxation without approval of a council	The three rights listed are protected by the Bill of Rights in the U.S. Constitution. The framers of the Constitution gave Congress, an elected body, the power to impose taxes.
English Bill of Rights • King or queen cannot cancel laws or impose taxes without Parliament's approval. • Free elections to Parliament and regular meetings of Parliament are guaranteed. • Excessive fines and cruel punishment for crimes are forbidden. • People have the right to complain to the king or queen in Parliament without being arrested. • Established the principle that government should be based on laws, not a ruler's decrees.	The U.S. system of government is based on the U.S. Constitution, which includes similar protections and guarantees and reflects the principle of rule of law.
Declaration of Independence • States that all men are created equal and have life, liberty, and the pursuit of happiness. Outlines these political principles: governments exist to protect people's rights, governments get their power from the consent of the governed, people have the right to overthrow a government that tramples on their rights.	The ideas that all people are created equal and that they have natural rights provided the basis for later Constitutional amendments that extended equal rights to minorities. Popular sovereignty—the idea that government gets its power from the people—is a basic principle of the U.S. Constitution.
Federalist Papers • Argued that the Constitution protects people's rights by weakening the power of any particular group so they cannot dominate. • Argued that the checks and balances system in the the Constitution would create a strong central government while still protecting states' rights.	These arguments helped get the Constitution ratified and are still important today in interpreting the Constitution.

Name ______________________ Date ______________

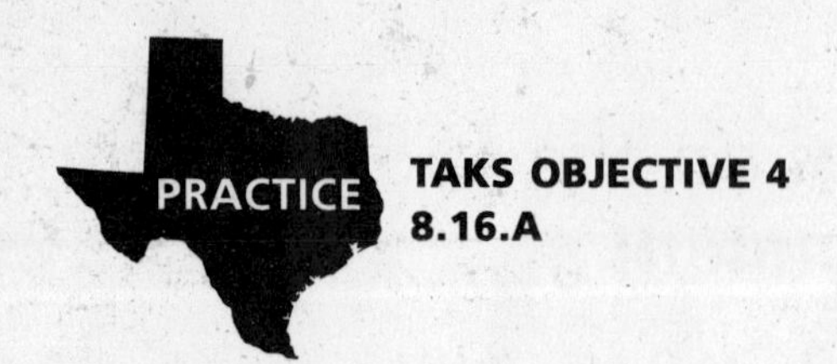

TAKS OBJECTIVE 4
8.16.A

Influences on the U.S. System of Government

Directions: Read the following questions and choose the best answer from among the four alternatives.

1 **Which of the following rights listed in the Magna Carta is part of the U.S. Bill of Rights?**

A Freedom of religion

B Freedom of speech

C Right to trial by jury

D Freedom of the press

2 **The English Bill of Rights established a principle that guides the U.S. system of government. This principle is that government should—**

F be based on the rule of law

G be based on federalism

H divide power among different groups

J include a parliament

3 **Which of the following basic principles of the U.S. Constitution was stated in the Declaration of Independence?**

A Federalism

B Popular sovereignty

C Checks and balances

D Separation of powers

4 **How do the Federalist Papers influence the operation of the U.S. government today?**

F They are used to amend the Constitution.

G They are used to justify federalism.

H They are used to interpret the Constitution.

J All of the above

Name ______________________________ Date ______________

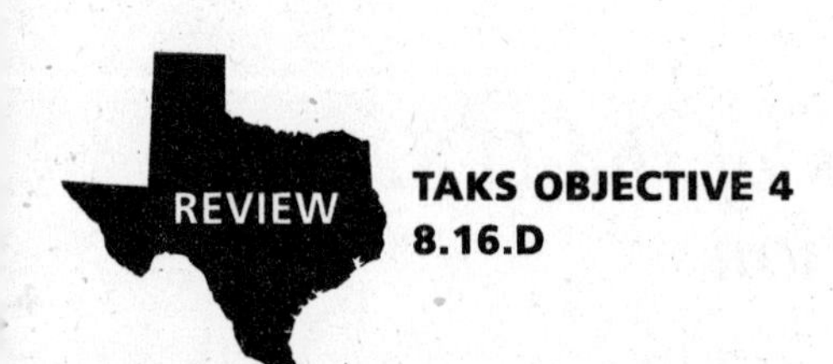

TAKS OBJECTIVE 4
8.16.D

Principles of the U.S. Constitution

Learning Objective Analyze how the U.S. Constitution reflects the principles of limited government, republicanism, checks and balances, federalism, separation of powers, popular sovereignty, and individual rights.

The U.S. Constitution is founded on the seven principles listed in the objective above. The chart below defines the first three principles and summarizes how the Constitution reflects each principle. (Page 59 covers the other four principles.) Review the chart to answer the questions on the next page.

Principle and Definition	How the Constitution Reflects the Principle
Limited Government restriction on the power of the government	• It spells out the powers that each branch of government has. For example, Congress has the power to pass laws, the president has the power power to execute those laws, and the judiciary has the power to interpret the laws.
Republicanism a form of government in which people elect representatives to make and carry out laws	• It states that members of Congress shall be elected by the people. • It guarantees each state a republican form of government
Checks and Balances a system of controls on the power of government in in which each branch of government checks the power of the other branches	• It states that Congress has the power to pass laws, but the president can refuse to sign a bill into law. • It gives the president the power to make treaties and appoint supreme court judges, but the Senate must approve these treaties and appointments. • It gives the Supreme Court the power to rule on on cases involving the Constitution, national laws, treaties, and states' conflicts. The Supreme Court court can decide that an act of Congress or the president is unconstitutional. • It gives Congress the authority to impeach and remove the president and federal judges.

Name ______________________________ Date ______________

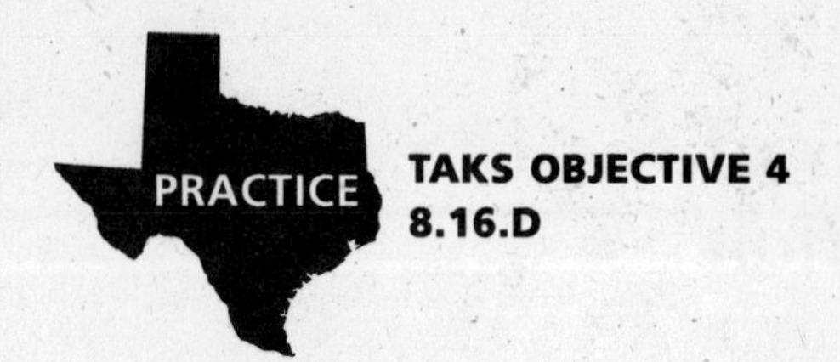

TAKS OBJECTIVE 4
8.16.D

Principles of the U.S. Constitution

Directions: Read the following questions and choose the best answer from among the four alternatives.

1 Which of the following is an example of the principle of republicanism in the U.S. Constitution?

A The president has the power to veto laws passed by Congress.

B The state or the people keep any powers not delegated to the federal government.

C The Supreme Court can declare a law unconstitutional.

D The people elect representatives to Congress.

2 An example of checks and balances in the U.S. Constitution is the provision that—

F each state is guaranteed a republican form of government

G the Senate must approve Supreme Court appointments made by the president

H the president commands the nation's armed forces

J All of the above

3 How does the U.S. Constitution reflect the principle of limited government?

A By spelling out the powers of each branch of government

B By identifying the powers denied to Congress and to the states

C By stating that the people or the states keep all rights not delegated to the national government

D All of the above

4 The Supreme Court can check the power of Congress or the president by—

F ruling that a law or act is unconstitutional

G impeaching a representative or the president

H vetoing a law

J withholding funds to enforce a law or presidential act

Name ______________________________ Date ______________

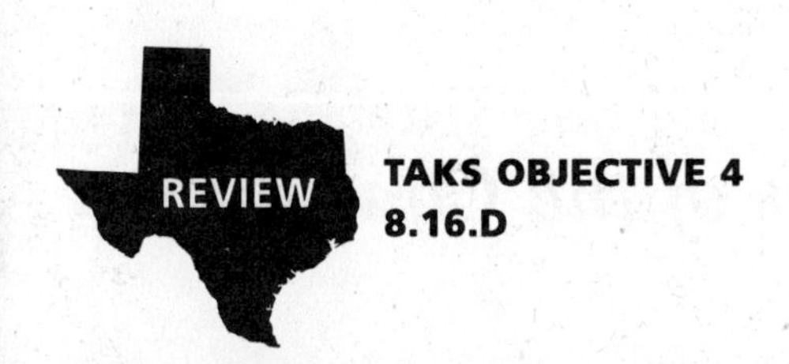

TAKS OBJECTIVE 4
8.16.D

Principles of the U.S. Constitution

Learning Objective Analyze how the U.S. Constitution reflects the principles of limited government, republicanism, checks and balances, federalism, separation of powers, popular sovereignty, and individual rights.

As you have learned, the U.S. Constitution is founded on the seven principles listed in the objective above. The chart below defines the last four principles and summarizes how the Constitution reflects each of these principles. Review the chart to answer the questions on the next page.

Principle and Definition	How the Constitution Reflects the Principle
Federalism a system of government in which the states and national government share powers	• It lists the powers of the national government and and the powers denied the states. • It states that powers not delegated to the national government should be retained by the states or by the people. • It states that national law is the supreme law. • It declares that states must honor one another's laws, records, and court rulings. • It requires the states to approve amendments.
Separation of Powers the division of basic government roles into different branches with no one branch having all the power	The first three articles of the Constitution state how powers are split among the three branches of. government. In general, Congress makes the laws, the president enforces them, and the judicial branch interprets the law. The president is the commander of the armed forces, but only Congress can declare war.
Popular Sovereignty The government gets its authority from the people and reflects their will.	• It states that the people will elect representatives. • It declares that the people or the states keep any any powers not delegated to the national government. • It guarantees all citizens the same rights and equal protection of the laws. • All citizens 18 years and older are allowed to vote.
Individual Rights liberties and privileges each citizen has	• The Bill of Rights guarantees a number of rights, including freedom of religion, speech, the press, and assembly. • Later amendments abolished slavery and extended voting.

Name ______________________ Date ____________

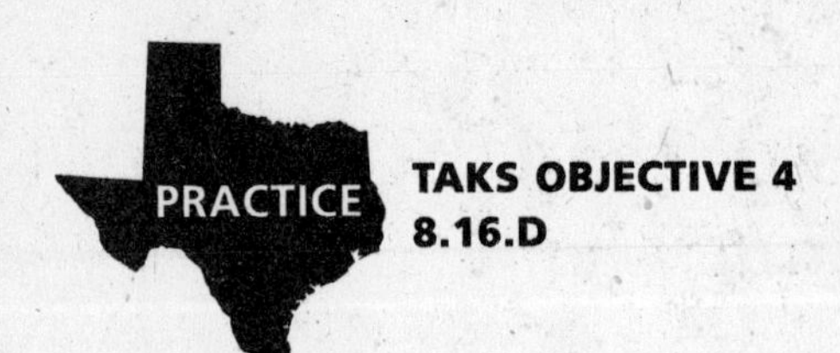

TAKS OBJECTIVE 4
8.16.D

Principles of the Constitution

Directions: Read the following questions and choose the best answer from among the four alternatives.

1 The U.S. Constitution promotes the principle of federalism by stating that—

A all powers not delegated to the national government are retained by the states or the people

B all citizens have the right to vote

C all citizens shall enjoy freedom of religion

D the president is the commander of the armed forces, but only Congress can declare war

2 The Constitution's division of the government into three branches with distinct powers reflects the principle of—

F individual rights

G popular sovereignty

H separation of powers

J federalism

3 Which of the following is not an individual right protected by the Constitution?

A Freedom of speech

B Equal protection under the law

C Right to vote

D Right to ignore laws you disagree with

4 Which of the following is an example of how the Constitution reflects the principle of popular sovereignty?

F All citizens 18 years and older are entitled to vote.

G Citizens elect representatives.

H The states or the people keep powers not delegated to the national government.

J All of the above

Name ____________________ Date ____________

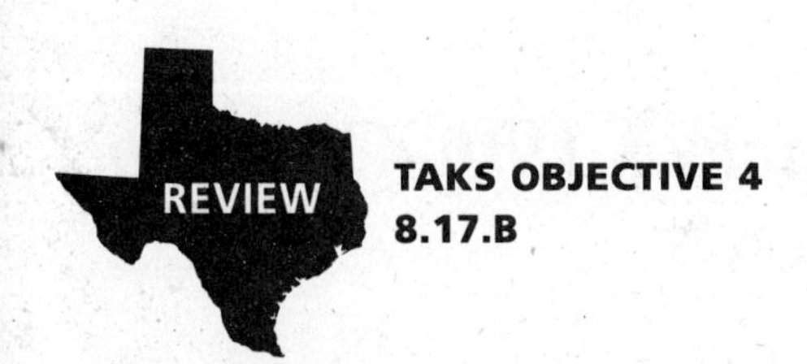

TAKS OBJECTIVE 4
8.17.B

The Impact of 19th-Century Amendments

Learning Objective Describe the impact of 19th-century amendments, including the 13th, 14th, and 15th amendments, on life in the United States.

The 13th, 14th, and 15th amendments are often called the Reconstruction Amendments because they were passed after the Civil War to grant rights to recently freed African Americans. Over the course of time, these amendments have served to protect the individual rights of not only African Americans but also women, the disabled, and other minority groups. In this way, they have contributed to the increased participation of all groups in American life. The text below summarizes these amendments and their impact on American life. Review the information to answer the questions on the next page.

13th Amendment (1865) End of Slavery

What it did: abolished slavery in the United States

Impact

- This amendment freed millions of enslaved people and permanently ended slavery in the United States.
- Many African Americans in the South left plantations, found jobs, reunited with their families, and started schools and churches. Eventually, some African Americans returned to plantations to work for wages or as sharecroppers.
- This amendment provided the legal basis for the supreme court to later outlaw other forms of enforced labor, which affected both African Americans and Mexicans in the Southwest.

14th Amendment (1868) Civil Rights

What it did: granted citizenship and equal protection of the laws to all persons born in the United States except Native Americans

Impact

- Although it was not immediately enforced throughout the United States, it later became the basis for court decisions that ended segregation.
- It provided the legal basis for many civil rights laws of the 20th century, such as those that prohibited job discrimination, required access to public places for the disabled, and prescribed equal resources for boys and girls in school athletics.

15th Amendment (1870) Right to Vote

What it did: Guaranteed that the right to vote could not be denied based on race, color, or previous enslavement.

Impact

- This amendment was designed to protect the voting rights of African Americans, and many African Americans did begin to vote after it was passed. However, some states set voter qualifications that kept African Americans from voting. Nevertheless, the amendment provided the legal basis for voting rights laws passed in the 1900s. After the Voting Rights Act of 1965 was passed, the number of African American voters increased greatly, and more African Americans were then elected to political office.
- It strengthened the women's drive to gain the right to vote.

Name ______________________________ Date ______________

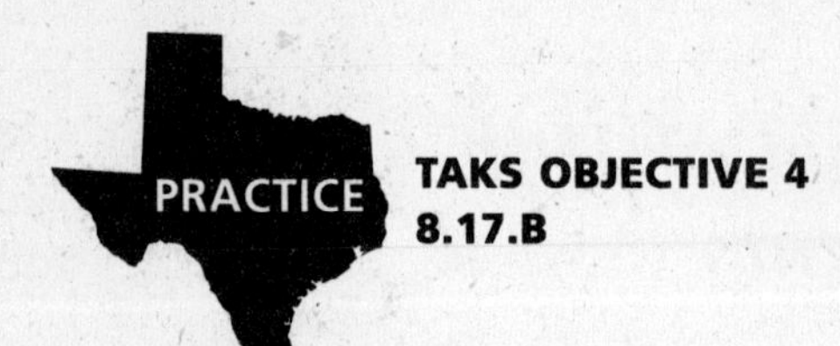

TAKS OBJECTIVE 4
8.17.B

The Impact of 19th-Century Amendments

Directions: Read the following questions and choose the best answer from among the four alternatives.

1 After the 13th Amendment abolished slavery in the United States, many African Americans in the South—

A left plantations and found jobs

B reunited with their families

C started schools and churches

D All of the above

2 Although it was not immediately enforced, the 14th Amendment eventually helped to end—

F segregation

G job discrimination

H sex discrimination in school athletics

J All of the above

3 Which of the following statements accurately reflects the main effect of the 15th Amendment?

A Many African Americans eventually began voting in local and national elections.

B It ensured that African Americans had equal representation in Congress.

C It gave women the right to vote.

D It removed all the barriers that kept African Americans from voting.

4 Which of the following was not an effect of the Reconstruction Amendments?

F They immediately ended discrimination against African Americans.

G They eventually led to increased participation of African Americans in the nation's political life.

H They eventually aided the cause of women's rights.

J They were used to protect the civil rights of many minority groups in the United States.

Name ____________________ Date ____________

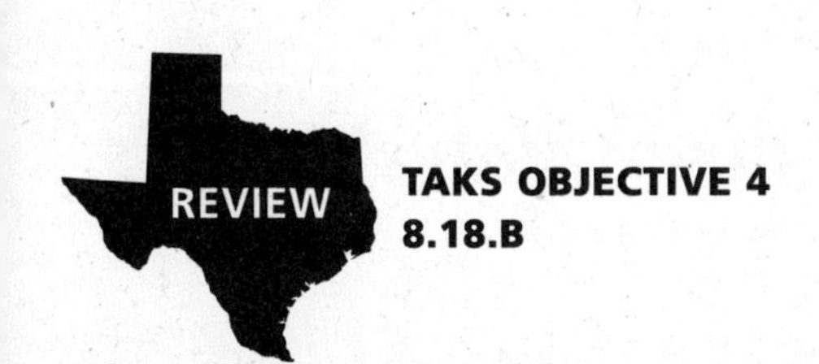

TAKS OBJECTIVE 4
8.18.B

Conflicts over States' Rights Issues

Learning Objective Describe the historical conflicts arising over the issue of states' rights, including the Nullification Crisis and the Civil War.

The issue of states' rights increasingly divided Americans, especially Northerners and Southerners, in the decades before the Civil War. It pitted those who favored a strong national government against those who defended the rights of the states. It was a major political issue from 1828, when the Nullification Crisis began, until the Civil War was fought to resolve it. The chart below provides background information and outlines the escalating argument in the Nullification Crisis, which lasted from 1828 to 1833. Review the chart before answering the questions on the next page.

Nullification Crisis

The crisis arose over the issue of tariffs.

South	North
Because its economy depended on foreign trade, the South opposed a federal bill that significantly raised tariffs. Vice-President John Calhoun of South Carolina proposed that a state had the right to nullify, or reject, a federal law that it considered unconstitutional.	President Andrew Jackson and Congressional leaders from the North opposed the doctrine of nullification. They believed that all states must obey federal laws. However, Congress reduced the tariffs to try to satisfy the South.
Action Taken	**Action Taken**
South Carolina thought the tariffs were still too high and nullified them. Its leaders voted to form an army and threatened to secede, or withdraw, from the Union.	Jackson made it clear that federal laws would be enforced, and Congress passed a compromise tariff that satisfied South Carolina and ended the crisis.

Name ______________________ Date ____________

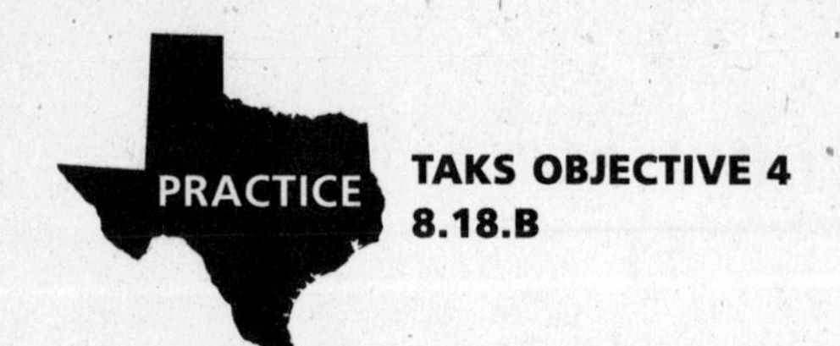

TAKS OBJECTIVE 4
8.18.B

Conflicts Over States' Rights Issues

Directions: Read the following questions and choose the best answer from among the four alternatives.

1 **The Nullification Crisis pitted those who favored a strong national government against—**

A those who favored no government

B those who favored strong state governments

C those who opposed slavery

D those who opposed secession

2 **The Nullification Crisis was sparked by the issue of—**

F slavery

G high tariffs

H freedom of speech

I land grants

3 **In the Nullification Crisis, South Carolina declared that states had the right to—**

A reject federal laws

B permit slavery

C nullify Native American claims to land

D issue their own money

4 **The Nullification Crisis could have led to the breakup of the Union because—**

F South Carolina threatened to secede

G South Carolina threatened the authority of the national government

H federal laws would have been meaningless if each state could decide not to obey them

I All of the above

Name ______________________________ Date ______________

TAKS OBJECTIVE 4
8.18.B

Conflicts Over States' Rights Issues

Learning Objective Describe the historical conflicts arising over the issue of states' rights, including the Nullification Crisis and the Civil War.

The issue of states' rights became so divisive that Americans fought the Civil War to resolve it. The chart below summarizes the conflict immediately leading up to the Civil War. Review the chart before answering the questions on the next page.

Conflict Leading up to the Civil War

The question of whether to allow slavery in the territories divided the North and the South for years.

South	North
The Southern states, which depended on slave labor to produce cotton, wanted slavery allowed in the territories and in new states formed from the territories. They did not want free states to become a majority in Congress.	The Northern states did not want slavery to expand. Abraham Lincoln, who opposed the expansion of of slavery into the territories, won the presidency in 1860.
Action Taken	**Action Taken**
The Southern states had threatened to secede if if Lincoln won the presidency. South Carolina seceded first, arguing that the states voluntarily joined the Union and had the right to leave it.	Mississippi, Florida, Alabama, Georgia, Louisiana, and Texas joined South Carolina in secession, and together they formed the Confederate States of of America. They adopted a constitution that supported states' rights and slavery.

Name ______________________________ Date ______________

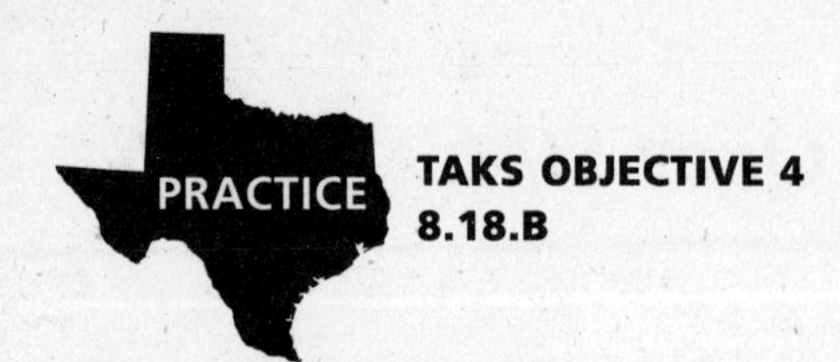

TAKS OBJECTIVE 4
8.18.B

Conflicts Over States' Rights Issues

Directions: Read the following questions and choose the best answer from among the four alternatives.

1 The main issue that divided the North and South in the years just before the Civil War was—

A how to breakup large plantations and redistribute land in the South

B whether to institute an income tax

C whether to allow slavery in the territories and in new states

D whether to allow new states to join the Union

2 Southerners were opposed to Lincoln's presidency because he—

F wanted to redistribute land in the South

G wanted to institute an income tax

H opposed the expansion of slavery into the territories and new states

J wanted to allow new states to join the Union

3 What argument did South Carolina use to justify seceding from the Union?

A The states had joined the Union voluntarily and so had the right to secede.

B The First Amendment to the Constitution guaranteed states the right to secede.

C The federal government was sovereign.

D The right to secession was an unalienable right.

4 Which of the following statements accurately reflects the North's position on secession?

F It was unconstitutional because the federal government, not the state governments, was sovereign.

G It was unconstitutional because the U.S. Constitution did not specifically give states this right.

H The states had the right to secede, but only when the federal government trampled on states' rights.

J The states had the right to secede because the U.S. Constitution did not specifically forbid it.

Name ______________________ Date ______________

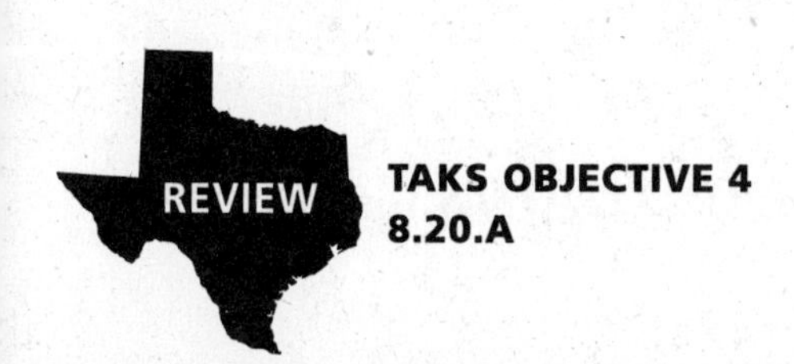

TAKS OBJECTIVE 4
8.20.A

Unalienable Rights

Learning Objective Define and give examples of unalienable rights.

The following chart provides a definition, examples, and discussion of unalienable rights. Review this chart before answering the questions on the next page.

Unalienable Rights	**Definition:** rights that can't be taken away
Examples	**Discussion**
• right to life • right to liberty • right to pursue happiness	The term unalienable rights comes from the Declaration of Independence, which states that they include the right to life, liberty, and the pursuit of happiness. The idea of unalienable rights comes from the English philosopher John Locke, who influenced Thomas Jefferson in writing the Declaration of of Independence. Locke wrote that all people possessed "the same natural rights of life, liberty, and property." According to Locke, these rights were God-given, and all people were equal in possessing them. Jefferson did not include the ownership of property as an unalienable right.

Name ______________________________ Date ______________

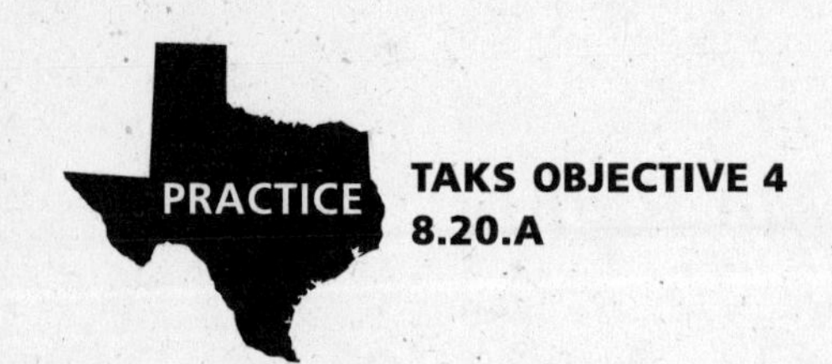

TAKS OBJECTIVE 4
8.20.A

Unalienable Rights

Directions: Read the following questions and choose the best answer from among the four alternatives.

1 Which of the following is the best definition of the term unalienable rights?

A Rights that aliens possess

B Rights that cannot be taken away

C Rights that are protected by written law

D Rights listed in the U.S. Constitution

2 Which of the following is an unalienable right identified in the Declaration of Independence?

F Life

G Liberty

H Pursuit of happiness

J All of the above

3 Another term for unalienable rights is—

A natural rights

B legal rights

C civil rights

D equal rights

4 Which of the following is a natural right that John Locke identified but that Thomas Jefferson did not include in the Declaration of Independence?

F Ownership of property

G Right to bear arms

H Freedom of assembly

J Freedom of the press

Name ______________________ Date ______________

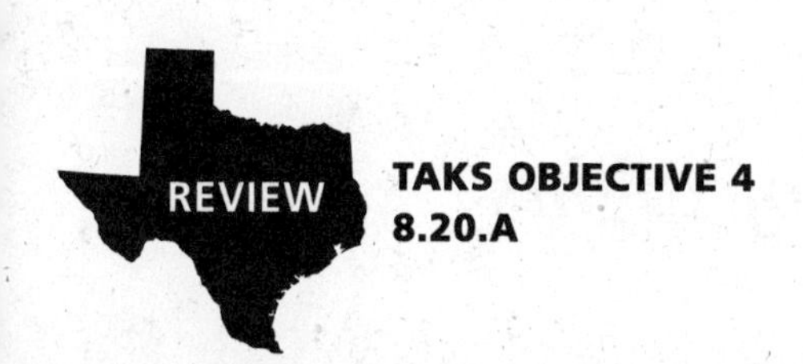

TAKS OBJECTIVE 4
8.20.A

The Bill of Rights

Learning Objective Summarize the rights guaranteed in the Bill of Rights.

The following chart summarizes the rights listed in the first ten amendments to the U.S. Constitution, which makeup the Bill of Rights. Review the chart before answering the questions on the next page.

Rights Guaranteed in the Bill of Rights

Amendment	Rights
One	• freedom of religion, speech, press, assembly, petition
Two	• State militias have the right to be armed.
Three	• The armed forces cannot house soldiers in people's homes unless it is approved by law.
Four	• The government cannot search or seize a person's property without a warrant, or written court order. • The warrant must specify the reason for the search and identify the people and property to be searched.
Five	• A person cannot be tried for a serious crime unless a grand jury rules that evidence exists for a trial. • A person cannot be tried for the same crime twice. • A person does not have to testify against himself or herself. • A person accused of a crime has the right to due process of law.
Six	• A person accused of a crime has the right to a quick and fair trial by jury in the state and district where the crime was committed. • A person has the right to be informed of the crime he or she is accused of, to be confronted with the witnesses against him or her, to be allowed to obtain witnesses in his or her favor, and to have the assistance of a lawyer.
Seven	• right to a jury trial in lawsuits over money, property, or injury valued at more than 20 dollars
Eight	• Courts cannot prescribe excessive bail, excessive fines, or cruel or unusual punishment.
Nine	• The listing of rights in the Constitution does not mean the people do not have other rights as well.
Ten	• Powers not given to the federal government by the Constitution belong to the states or the people.

Name ______________________________ Date ______________

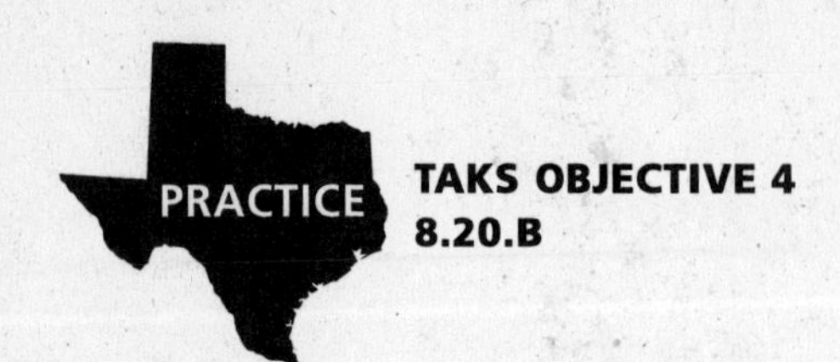

TAKS OBJECTIVE 4
8.20.B

The Bill of Rights

Directions: Read the following questions and choose the best answer from among the four alternatives.

1 Which of the following rights are guaranteed by the First Amendment in the Bill of Rights?

A Freedom of religion

B Freedom of speech

C Freedom of the press

D All of the above

2 Which of the following situations would not be protected by the Bill of Rights?

F A group of citizens hold a meeting to protest a proposed law

G A citizen refuses to allow a police officer to search his or her home because the officer has no warrant

H A person accused of a crime refuses to testify against himself or herself

J A person disobeys a law because he or she does not like it

3 The Bill of Rights states that a person accused of a crime has the right to—

A due process of law

B trial by a judge

C a trial within one week

D refuse a trial

4 Which of the following is not a right guaranteed by the Bill of Rights to a person accused of a crime?

F The right to be represented by a lawyer

G The right to a jury trial in the state and district where the crime occurred

H Freedom from having to testify against oneself

J The right to remain free until convicted of a crime

Name ______________________ Date ______________

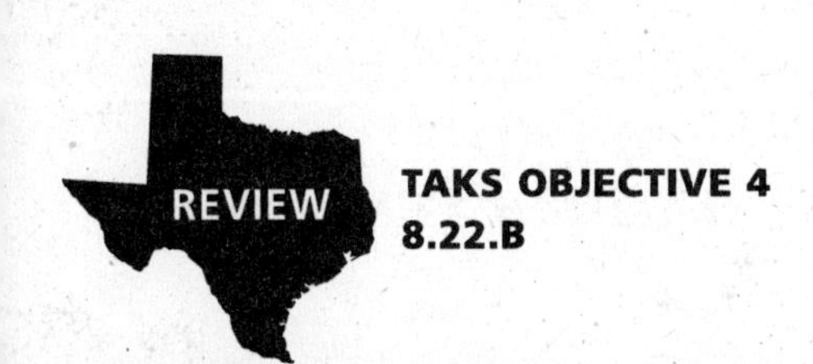

Free Speech and Press

Learning Objective Describe the importance of free speech and press in a democratic society.

The chart below outlines why free speech and press are important in a democracy. Review the chart before answering the questions on the next page.

Proposition	Supporting Reasons
Free speech and press are essential in a democracy.	• In a democracy, the people rule. In order to rule, they must be informed. They need access to information and differing viewpoints to decide on the best policies. • In a democracy, the government reflects the will of the people. Government officials need to know what people want in order to carry out their will. • Freedom of speech and the press promotes the exchange of information, ideas, and opinions. • Free speech and a free press both serve as checks on the power of government. Government officials know that their actions will be publicized and that they will be held accountable for their actions.

Name ______________________ Date ______________

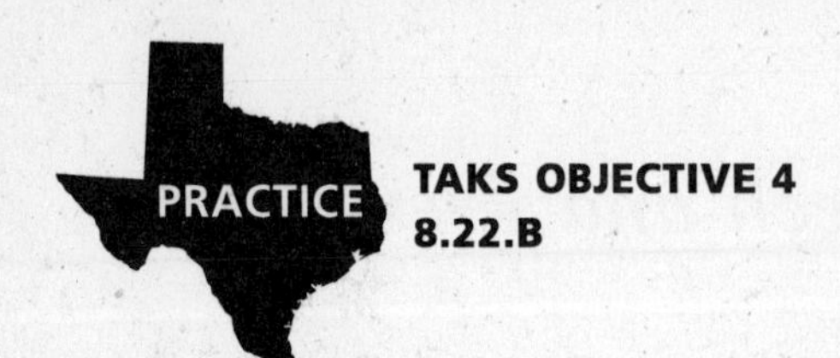

TAKS OBJECTIVE 4
8.22.B

Free Speech and Press

Directions: Read the following questions and choose the best answer from among the four alternatives.

1 A democracy depends on free speech and press because this form of government is intended to reflect—

A the opinions of the most educated members of society

B the will of the people

C the opinions of the media

D the best ideas of leaders in science, business, and education

2 Which of the following statements best expresses the role of a free press in a democratic society?

F It promotes the exchange of information, ideas, and opinions and serves as a check on the power of government.

G It informs the people about the government's policies and plans.

H It informs the government about the people's opinions.

J It allows minorities to express their viewpoints.

3 How does free speech and a free press aid the operation of a democracy?

A By helping people make informed decisions

B By helping to inform government officials about what people want

C By helping to make government officials accountable to the people

D All of the above

4 Which of the following would be a likely result if a democracy did not allow free speech and free press?

F People would only learn information that government officials chose to share.

G The government would have more control over people's lives.

H The government would not reflect the will of the people and would not be a democracy.

J All of the above